THE EVENING & THE MORNING
A Liberation Primer On The Creation Story

Alvin C. Bernstine

© 2019. Alvin C. Bernstine.

No part of this book may be reproduced or transmitted in any form, by any means, electronic or mechanical, including photocopying, recording, or by any information storage or retrieval system without the express permission in writing from the author.

ISBN: 978-0-9767020-6-1

Table of Contents

Acknowledgment v

Foreword vii

Preface - Context Matters ix

CHAPTER 1
Hermeneutics Matter 1

CHAPTER 2
The Creation Story Matters 18

CHAPTER 3
The Evening and The Morning Matters 26

CHAPTER 4
The First Day: 33
New Beginnings for People Who Need Them

CHAPTER 5
The Second Day: 48
Faith in the Firmament

CHAPTER 6
The Third Day: 59
The Let-Be God in a Make-Be World

CHAPTER 7
The Fourth Day: 71
Lights in the Firmament

Chapter 8
   The Fifth Day: 81
   The Over-And-Under God

Chapter 9
   The Sixth Day: 91
   Just Like God

Chapter 10
   The Seventh Day: 107
   A Time for God

Acknowledgment

I am grateful.

I am grateful to God for the wonderful opportunity to put thoughts to pen and paper. My journey with writing has been a challenge, beginning with a woefully inadequate primary education in the Oakland Public School systems. My writing journey, however, was greatly enhanced by some amazing educators, such as the late John Gardenhire at Laney College; Helen Benjamin at Bishop College; the late Dr. Kelly Miller Smith, Sr. at Vanderbilt Divinity School; and the late Dr. Samuel Dewitt Proctor at United Theological Seminary. The encouragement I received from Dr. Amos Jones, Jr., while in Nashville, Tennessee was invaluable. His fluid pen continues to inspire me to unapologetically write about the Christian faith from a black church perspective. Dr. J. Alfred Smith, Sr., Pastor Emeritus of Allen Temple Baptist Church, Oakland, has modeled for me the blessings of being a writing pastor. Even now he sows into me words of wisdom and encouragement.

I am grateful for Joyce Evans, whom I have never physically met, yet through the genius of cyberspace she has provided me invaluable technical and publishing assistance for over 10 years. It has been a joy working with her. I know that as she assists me, she also is giving creative expression to the publishing ministry within her.

I am grateful for the wonderful people of the Bethlehem Missionary Baptist Church of Richmond, California, who afford me opportunity, experience, and time to test my rambling thoughts on them.

I am grateful for Dr. Renita Weems, who interrupted her full life, to contribute her incredible wisdom to this publication. Her amazing academic gifts in no way eclipse her love for God's people. I graciously receive her gift of assessment to this writing as a gift of love. Thank you Dr. Weems.

Finally, I am grateful to God for gifting me with the wonderful woman who shares my life as friend, confidante, advisor, preaching mentee, ministry colleague, soul mate, and lover – the inimitable Diana Becton. Diana has been the bright morning who consistently follows my dark evenings with compassionate presence, hopeful perspective, and gentle nudging.

I am grateful.

Foreword

To a scholar of Hebrew Scriptures like myself, the idea of a book of sermons about the Creation Story/ies in Genesis may strike one as a bit odd. What modern black preacher expounds from Genesis 1-3 except to reinscribe tired, ill-informed notions about creation, nature, patriarchy, domination, and gender roles (i.e., namely, women's complementary, but inferior, role in the world)? Who trudges through the tohu wabohu (chaos) of primeval history in Genesis to find meaning for today except someone advocating pre-modern beliefs about time and eternity? None of these things occupy any dominant place of interest in this book of sermons. Rev. Alvin Bernstine invites his readers to look anew at the Creation story/ies of Genesis for models of the church's witness for liberation, resistance, critique, and transformative engagement with the created order. Bernstine is convinced that Creation is a counter point to the darkness, chaos, and emptiness that characterizes much of modern day human existence.

Bernstine is explicit about his commitment as a preacher and pastor to make the Bible speak to the complex concerns of the African-American community. "The Evening and the Morning" is evidence of his effort to be in conversation with discourses in black and liberation scholarship to develop a theology of pastoral care and hermeneutic of scriptural interpretation that affirm the significance of black people's God-talk, survival, and praxis in the world.

Finally, the average thoughtful preacher has shelves of books probably by technicians of homiletics on how to craft better sermons. What preachers struggling weekly to hear from God need more of are more books by practitioners of preaching who struggle with the task of interpreting the Bible and keeping it alive to congregations bored with prognostication. Books like the one you are holding in your hands are helpful resources because they offer readers, both clergy and lay, a glimpse into the practitioner at work at his craft. "The Evening and the Morning" is a testament to the wisdom, the wrestling, and the witness of someone who for forty-plus years has sought weekly (and in between) to bring head and heart to the vocation to which he has been called by God, the call to preaching the good news of the gospel to the poor, the imprisoned, the brokenhearted, and those longing to be free.

Renita J. Weems, Ph.D.
Pentecost Season 2019

Preface

Context Matters

Quite early in my formal matriculation as a "would-be preacher," I learned that "a text without a context is a pretext." When first I heard it I didn't fully understand it, but understood enough to know that a written text is best understood when the context from which it was written is faithfully and studiously explored. This went against the grain of a well-used thoughtless saying once popular among my denominational circles. Preachers and teachers would forcefully proclaim, "If the Bible said it, I believe it, and that settles it!" (This saying would later be reduced to "The Bible said it, and that settles it!") We were being encouraged to shut down our brains and just accept whatever the Bible said without exegetical inquiry, historical location, cultural understanding, or hermeneutical conclusions. No thought was to be given to the socio-economic-political verities of a text's world. In a sense, the people of the text were ignored and the text was reduced to a presumptuous exchange between the reader and God. Therefore, most of the preaching and teaching being espoused went forth text without context.

As we witness governmental leaders justify inhumane policies and practices with loose usage of biblical texts, we are being forced to asked, "Did the Bible mean that?" We hear the dismay of even the most marginal Christian expressing concern that a text is being taken out of context. Context matters so much that we cannot risk ignoring the fact that even non-biblical text, such as the U.S. Constitution, must forever be viewed through the query of context. As a community pastor, obligated to teach the Bible, I developed a template to follow that insists that students understand that every text was written by somebody who was writing to someone about something going on somewhere affecting people at a specific time. Therefore, it behooved the responsible preacher and/or teacher to give due diligence in finding out who the somebody was and to whom was the writing for and what was going on in that place at that specific time to provoke the writing of the text.

The Creation Story is probably one of the best-known stories within the biblical text. Yet, its relevance should not be presumed, or its meaning assumed. Some questions should be asked. Is there a context for it? Or, does the text self-manifest without aid of contextual realities? Why the poetic stanza "the evening and the morning"? If possible to locate, what was going on in the world that provokes the need for a Creation Story and to have each day marked with "the evening and the morning"? I believe such questions are answered through the exploration of context and the insights derived therein are fraught with hermeneutical possibilities.

Admittedly I did not always consider the hermeneutical importance of the Creation Story. I believed it to be what I had been told it was, the story of "how" the world was created – that and nothing more. Even when exposed to a valid alternative perspective, I chose to comfortably live in the literalistic space where "the Bible said it, and that settles it!" How painfully limiting an assumed hermeneutical lens can be! We can literally see in blind ways.

As one who longed to consider the Bible as a liberating tool for people of faith and good will, for years I ignored what the Creation Story might mean for people who yearned and desperately needed liberating perspectives. While the "mis-education" of black people is legend, I hold that we have to assume some responsibility for ignoring the truths that have been set before us. A sliver of truth can swing wide the imaginative exegete to produce a liberating hermeneutic and/or transformative interpretation of the text. This becomes more pressing for a people who've longed understood that a word out of context could indeed be a pretext. A noted quote from the prophetess, Maya Angelou, when asked about what to teach children; she said, "Tell the truth, first to yourself." Hermeneutics in context is telling the truth first to yourself.

To that end we consider how hermeneutics matter.

CHAPTER 1

HERMENEUTICS MATTER

During a recent class on Womanist Preaching, the profound and provocative instructor Dr. Donna Allen challenged us to preach with the intent to move people from orthodoxy (right belief) to orthopraxis (right conduct). She argued that preaching ought to call Christians to more than just believing something about Jesus, but to actually doing something with Jesus. I interpreted her to mean that responsible preaching should call us to doing something in radical obedience to Jesus. He did, in fact, call us to follow him.

Contrary to the domesticated posture of much of American Christianity, following Jesus is radical! We are called to follow him in ways that manifest the radical love we have for God and one another. He asked us to deny ourselves so that the fruit of obedience would be radically realized among those whose lives have been ravaged by oppressive systems and constructs, particularly the economically disadvantaged. As a citizen of an oppressed and marginalized people, Jesus invited us into a loyalty greater than the suffocating impositions of a colonizing power that is often sustained by a theology of imperialism, which reduces most churches to being what Walter Brueggemann identifies as "chapels of the empire."

Such radical love includes assuming a space of redemptive suffering as a means of experiencing resurrection realities as life-affirming resistance to death-dealing social constructs. Obedience to the call, doing what he commands, constitutes the basic responses of orthopraxis in following Jesus.

> Many of our churches are filled with people who assume right belief, but do little to right the pervasive wrongs of the world and the invasive wrongs in our heads.

Unfortunately, the orthodoxy emphases of the dominant perspectives and practices of American Christianity preclude orthopraxis. Other than an exaggerated focus on sexual immorality, self-enrichment, and personal piety, our pulpits and Bible studies have become repositories for right belief while neglecting right conduct. As one preacher noted, "We say more about the things he said the least about, and say the least about the things he said the most about."[1]

As a result, many of our churches are filled with people who assume right belief but do little to right the pervasive wrongs of the world and the invasive wrongs in our heads. Is it any wonder that the Church is habitually the last entity to arrive at the battlefields of injustice? It seems as if the Church has adopted the compromising posture assumed when surrendering to what Howard Thurman identified as "the three hounds of hell that track the trail of the disinherited."[2] The spiritually debilitating

---

1. William Barber in the foreword of Wilson-Hartgrove, Jonathan, Reconstructing the Gospel: Finding Freedom from Slaveholder Religion (Denver Grove, IL, Intervarsity Press, 2018)
2. Thurman, Howard, *Jesus And the Disinherited*, (Boston: Beacon Press), 1949, p. 13

forces of fear, hypocrisy, and hatred have not relented in their quest to conquer the human spirit, particularly the spirit of those bound within the webs of oppressive constructs. Orthodoxy deprived of orthopraxy has diluted the preaching experience into nothing more than oratorical gibberish, seasoned with colonial theology and commoditized epistemology. Paul considered such preaching as "speaking into the air" (1 Cor. 14:9, NKJV).

It strikes me that the central challenge for moving from orthodoxy to orthopraxis is a matter of hermeneutic, or biblical, interpretation. How we interpret the Bible matters! Often lost in the drama of Black religion is the continuing stronghold of centuries of biblical interpretation that encourages white supremacy and favors black oppression. While not expected from white pulpits, very few preachers within the Black Church consistently give attention to the oppressive legacy attached to the teaching and practice of Western Christianity, nor lift up the voices of resistance replete within the biblical text.

Prophetic preaching has been reduced to sensationalized fortune-telling, limited to individualized desires and personal aggrandizement. As a consequence, we have not come close to exorcising the demons of slave religion that distorted the biblical text for the sole purpose of perpetuating white supremacy and sustaining black inferiority. The oppressive toxicity of Western Christianity maintains a stronghold throughout America, and continues to subvert prophetic ministry among the most marginalized.

After years of black protest and resistance, we have not begun to hold white denominations, or their seminaries, accountable for the continued advancement of an oppressive understanding of the Christian faith. In fact, many black preachers have found academic solace in obtaining pseudo degrees from white institutions stamped with the seal of oppressive orthodoxy that does nothing more than further the colonialization of black minds. The inexplicable commitment to the theologically unfiltered religion of our enslavement has rendered impotent many who lead and preach within the Black Church. As a consequence, we are unable to liberate ourselves and provide a more liberating understanding of the Christian faith. The overemphasis on orthodoxy—in particular, a distorted orthodoxy—deprives us of the hermeneutical ingenuity to move us into any liberatory praxis.

A perfect example of this is evident in the proud display of a document in most African-American Baptist churches called "The Church Covenant," prominently displayed as a statement on faith, of which very few can justify or locate its origin. The Baptist Covenant opens up with the orthopraxis lines, "Having been led as we believe . . ."

Interestingly, the Baptist Covenant's emphasis on belief focuses the believers on intra-congregational behavior, and not on liberating communal engagement. While an argument might be made for its focus on the dynamics of healthy community behavior, I'm not convinced it describes a community that I would knowingly join or enthusiastically want to be part of.

The adherents to the Baptist Covenant community seem a bit too morally sanitized to effectuate grace, let alone generate any humor toward the drama of human existence.

Personally, I prefer faith with tension, struggle, mystery, and with a generous portion of humor. Being human is tense, filled with struggle, complex; and if the popularity of comedians is an indicator, it is also quite humorous. Moreover, the Covenant emphasizes behaviors that essentially promote how to get along in church, to the exclusion of how to change and make better the world. It seems to me that personal piety and denominational fidelity serve as the primary objectives of this hermeneutically distorted document.

If we, of the Baptist persuasion, faithfully conformed to the Baptist Covenant (as so few do), it would set us up for a lifetime of pious engagement of the biblical text to the neglect of prophetic responsibility. Martin Luther King, Jr., a Baptist preacher, could never have used the Baptist Covenant as a literary tool to advocate for Civil Rights, racial justice, and economic equity. Even a casual consideration of the ministry and teachings of Jesus clearly suggests that he was concerned with greater things than how to be a good "church" person. The inaugural proclamation of his ministry (Luke 4:16–21) as well as its eschatological consummation (Matt. 25:31–46), are textual bookends of ministry to the least of these.

Moreover, the ministry of Jesus disrupted traditional religious orthodoxy and provoked the ire of religious leadership. Jesus called us to follow him in obedience to the radical claims of the kingdom of God, not religious orthodoxy. The kingdom of God, for Jesus, was antithetical to the kingdoms of this world, including the oppressive construct to come known as the United States of America.

I contend that the pathway to responsible biblical hermeneutics demands a respect for the world and the justice intent of its original audience. Without getting bogged down in the jargon of biblical criticism, the fact of a text being communicated from a context is generally assumed. However, we are not always faithful to such an understanding when it comes to the biblical text. Many of us choose to ignore that what we say and how we say it is always determined by where we are and what's going on with where we are. Consequently, we tend to impose, or assume, meanings alien to the world of author and audience.

C. John Collins provides a simple but adequate image of how a text is communicated.

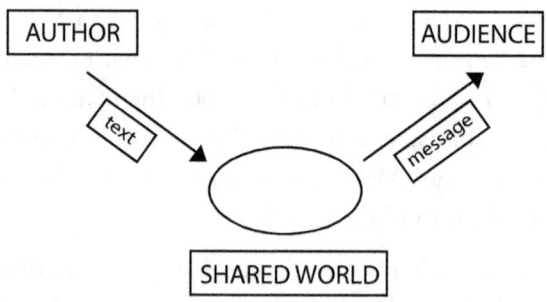

Both author and audience share a common worldview from which the text emerges and the message is understood. Collins insists that "we have not really apprehended the act of communication until we have considered this interaction."[3]

Along with context is the understanding that the historicity, or the worldview, of a text is grounded in socio-political realities. Something about how a people are living makes them say (or write) whatever they are saying (or writing), as well as how it is being read and received. I found the image provided in the Drama of Scripture[4] helpful in illustrating the historicity of the biblical text.:

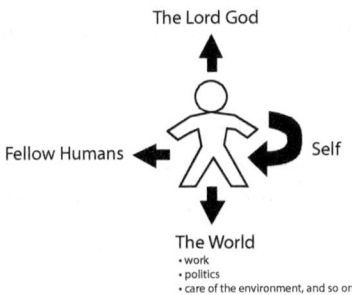

Communication is always contextual, and best understood by discerning what can be known about the context. While the meandering journey of biblical interpretation travels through many diverse perspectives, the ultimate objective of every hermeneutical pursuit is for the truths of the Bible to be responsibly

---

3. Collins, C.J., *Reading Genesis Well*, (Grand Rapids: Zondervan, 2018) p. 90.
4. Bartholomew, Craig G., Goheen, Michael, The Drama of Scripture, (Grand Rapids: Baker Academic, 2004, 2104) p. 42

applied to contemporary life. Thus, the hermeneutical quest is always to discern how what was communicated then impacts and influences what's going on now.

I considered a few definitions of the term *hermeneutics* and found that all held a commitment to studying the biblical text that leads to understanding in a world different from the world from whence the texts were originally written and heard. Some of those definitions are as follows:

Hermeneutics is the "art of understanding and making oneself understood."[5] According to this definition, hermeneutics is a process of understanding because of what is understood, particularly about the community and context of the assumed authors and recipients.

"For the preacher, hermeneutics is the art of placing the biblical text into conversation with contemporary life in order to arrive at something significant to say on Sunday morning."[6] Such a conversation responsibly connects the world then with the world now.

The Concise Encyclopedia of Preaching by Willimon & Lischer says Hermeneutics "refers to the method and techniques used to make a text understandable in a world different from the one in which the text originated." The methodology of hermeneutics acknowledges the differences in context as the gateway

---

5. *Zimmerman, Hermeneutics*. A Short Introduction (Oxford, Oxford University Press, 2015)
6. McClure, *Preaching Words*. 1434 Key Terms in Homiletics (Louisville, KY, Westminster John Knox, 2007)

to identifying the similarities in context. What is known about the world then opens up possibilities of connecting with the world we know now.

"Hermeneutics describes the task of explaining the meaning of the Scriptures."[7] Meaning represents a primal human longing that emerges from lived tensions within a prospective milieu. Scripture, as any other medium of communication, locates meaning among time-bound communities. Consequently, meaning must come from what was meant to those who originally authored and received the text.

"Hermeneutics provides the means of understanding the Scriptures and for applying that meaning responsibly."[8] Any application of Scripture must include some understanding of how it was originally appropriated among those to whom the text was intended, as well as how it was intended to be applied. A healthy place for any hermeneutical enterprise is to accept the humbling position of a secondary recipient. In other words, we were not the original people to read/hear the biblical text.

In the idiom of the African-American urban experience, hermeneutics is the complex effort to communicate the biblical text in ways that the people "understand where I'm [the preacher] coming from." Understanding what a person is saying is clearest when considering the person's social location.

---

7. Klein, Blomberg, and Hubbard, *Introduction to Biblical Interpretation*.
8. Ibid.

After 40 years of preaching, most of which was connected to serious efforts toward scholarship, I endeavor to offer the following definition: Hermeneutics is the artful and disciplined engagement of understanding the biblical text in ways that facilitate the text to be understood and appropriated in contemporary life.

Allow me to unpack the definition. First of all, hermeneutics as **artful** implies something as having aesthetic value, power, and function. Hermeneutics is a literary aesthetic that imaginatively engages the biblical text. Embedded within every text is an imagination that seeks to convey a response to a lived experience, often expressed in uncommon discourse. The text is not everyday speech. It is faith talk seeking to convey a hopeful alternative to an oppressive hegemony. A central task of the interpreter is to further the aesthetic journey in ways that respect the original authors and invites the current readers and/or hearers to consider reality differently. Through responsible hermeneutics, an alternative lens is provided that reimagines the world as if it truly is God's world, and God matters greatly enough to impact life profoundly.

> Hermeneutics is the artful and disciplined engagement of understanding the biblical text in ways that facilitate the text to be understood and appropriated in contemporary life.

As a **discipline**, hermeneutics commits to a systematic approach that objectively explores the biblical text. Critical to biblical interpretation is a high regard and respect for the biblical text, over and apart from personal and subjective preferences. Such regard demands that we respect the world and the words of the people who authored the text, as well as those who first encountered and received the text.

To respect the text, we submit to the rigors of responsible biblical scholarship and not just accept the views of those who have historically oppressed us. We are encouraged to develop the necessary tools to work with texts in ways that spiritually cultivate our ministry situations.

Finally, we bring the results of such scholarship to **engage** faith in ways that embolden transformative ministry that gives birth to hope and life. Without the engagement of faith, we risk fantasizing and resigning to an impotent romanticizing of the biblical text void of any social or personal consequence. Such an approach compromises the faith into becoming what Marx called an "opiate of the masses,"[9] anesthetizing people from their reality.

Hermeneutics engages the text. It pulls the reader or interpreter into the text so that he or she experiences the world of the text as it impacts the way he or she experiences his or her own world. While it should be stated that one's experience of

---

9. Marx, Karl, *"A Contribution to the Critique of Hegel's Philosophy of Right"*, Deutsch-Franzosiche, Feb., 1884.

the text's world is always limited, it is also always impactful. James Sanders noted that the "the reader is a major factor in how Scripture is read."[10]

I don't believe we can ever know the full detail of how the original readers engaged the text, but we do accept the fact that the text was engaged in ways that brought faith alive and reshaped an oppressive worldview. The text must impact the reader or interpreter by allowing him or her a perspective of how the text might have functioned. Moreover, the functionality of the text invites a faith response that is consistent with the world the text initially addressed. Cultural and societal apparatus may change throughout the ages, but human nature tends to remain constant. Biblical texts are essentially human responses to divine encounters that negotiate and challenge cultural or social apparatus.

Sanders further noted a triangular aspect of encountering the text: "1) the text in its complexity, created by the author/s in antiquity; 2) the sociopolitical situations of which the text arose and was later read and reread until it achieved a stable textual form; and 3) the hermeneutic used by the various contributors to the text as well as the hermeneutic of later readers."[11] All three of the above factors must be faithfully considered in order to understand, appreciate, and appropriate the intent of a text.

---

10. Sanders, James A., *The Monotheizing Process: Its Origins and Development*, (Eugene: Cascade Books, 2014), p. 2
11. Ibid, p. 2

Also critical to responsible interpretation is to make the text live in the world of the interpreter, and not limit its life to the past. A sainted senior sister within our congregation, Ruth Marshall, instinctively appropriates Sanders' academically refined observations. Mother Marshall produces amazingly insightful interpretations of the text because she reads the text until she sees herself running across the pages. Responsible hermeneutics is not nostalgia or pietistic reflections of the past. Neither is it an attempt to control people with doctrinal particularities that advocate institutional authoritarianism. Hermeneutics is an exegetical adventure exploring an ancient text and allowing its voice to be heard in a modern world. To the extent that the text can speak contemporaneously its ancient message can be obediently followed and the faith community can be more creatively formed and nurtured. We hermeneutically seek to see ourselves "running across the pages."

In this writing, I attempt to give witness to some of the things I have observed during an amazing life of preaching and teaching the biblical text. To begin, I have been privileged with the awesome honor of considering, preparing, and preaching the biblical text for over forty years, most of it as a pastor. The weekly responsibilities of preaching from the biblical text have challenged me to consider the biblical text in uncommon says. From my early days of preaching, I considered the Bible as offering more than the parroted expressions of tamed religion. While I did not always understand the implications of it, I took Jesus serious when he "opened the book, He found the place where it was written: The Spirit of the Lord is upon me, because He has anointed me to preach the gospel to the poor; He has sent me to heal the brokenhearted, to proclaim liberty to the captives, and recovery of sight to the blind, to set at liberty those who are oppressed; to proclaim the acceptable year of the Lord" (Luke 4:15b–19)

I must mention that for me, preaching and teaching has never been a solo act. Along this journey I have had the exposure, inclusive of friendships, to some of the most amazing preachers in three generations: the inimitable great generation before me, the formidable generation of which I am part, and the incredible millennial generation that follows me. The intergenerational genius of some amazingly responsible hermeneutics have not only informed my thinking, but encouraged and inspired me to think outside the box.

I also took seriously a life journey that began and remains connected with an oppressed and marginalized people. Betraying the cultural exigencies of who I was and where I came from was never an option. While I had ministry options, I instinctively understood that faith had to be lived out in the world from which I was historically and socially located. I found innately repulsive the thought of being a theological Uncle Tom who merely parrots the distortions of our oppressors. The dogged commitment to make the Bible speak to the complex concerns of the African-American community has persisted throughout my preaching lifetime. Locating resources and perspectives consistent with my hermeneutical instincts and pursuits remains a challenge because unfortunately, many interpretations have been culturally unashamed in perpetuating racial and gender biases. Yet embracing the black experience provided a perspective that forced me to see the text in ways that countered the spiritually castrating views commonly espoused.

Moreover, constructing, delivering, and now teaching preaching from a liberating perspective has been a primary source of ministry inspiration. Admittedly, being lured into the life-generating world of the biblical text has often been seductive. When rooted in its context biblical truth can often be shocking! Allowing the text an opportunity to be heard and experienced as an authentic voice from the margins shapes, inspires, and motivates sermonic struggles. The intersectionality of the Written Word and the Living Word provide the exegetical anvil from which we hermeneutically wrestle and emerge. After four decades I remain convinced, as did the early believers, that "the Word became flesh and dwelt among us."[12]

---

12. John 1:14

DISCUSSION MATTERS

I share the experience where Dr. Donna Allen challenged us to preach with the intent to move people from orthodoxy to orthopraxis.

1. What is meant by "orthodoxy"?
2. What is meant by "orthopraxis"?
3. I mentioned that contrary to the domesticated posture of much of American Christianity, following Jesus is radical! What are some of the radical positions, or actions taken by Jesus?
4. Spend some time unpacking the following quote.

Orthodoxy deprived of orthopraxy has diluted the preaching experience into nothing more than oratorical gibberish, seasoned with colonial theology and commoditized epistemology.

5. What does it mean? Do you agree? If not, why not?
6. Consider the following statement:
7. "Many black preachers have found academic solace in obtaining pseudo degrees from white institutions stamped with the seal of oppressive orthodoxy that does nothing more than further the colonialization of black minds."
8. What does it mean? Do you agree? If not, why not?
9. What are your thoughts on the Baptist Covenant?

10. What is meant by the assertion that "the pathway to responsible biblical hermeneutics demands a respect for the world and the justice intent of its original audience?"

A HERMENEUTICAL EXERCISE

Using John C. Collins template on page 6, locate a scripture of your choice and determine who is the "author" and "audience"; what is the "shared world-view?"

What are your thoughts on the author's definition of hermeneutics?

Hermeneutics is the artful and disciplined engagement of understanding the biblical text in ways that facilitate the text to be understood and appropriated in contemporary life.

How would your preaching or teaching be communicated if you were committed to the following?:

Allowing the text an opportunity to be heard and experienced as an authentic voice from the margins shapes, inspires, and motivates my sermonic struggles.

CHAPTER 2

THE CREATION STORY MATTERS

As earlier alluded to, I endeavor to begin an experiment of responsible biblical interpretation at the beginning. The beginning, in this instance, means at the canonical beginning of the biblical text. Genesis, as book of beginnings, decisively sets the hermeneutical trajectory of the biblical text. I contend that the opening story of the Bible sets the stage for how the Bible has been esteemed and interpreted on the one hand, or literally consumed and hermeneutically distorted on the other. While there are many views of the Creation Story, from science-based theories to exegetically based interpretations, none are politically or ideologically innocent and benign. Every biblical interpretation in Western Christianity is fraught with political and ideological agendas, most of which uphold and sustain an oppressive status quo. Two insightful scholars opined that we are guilty of misreading scripture because of the cultural blinders imposed by Western eyes.[13]

I wholeheartedly disagree, and in fact, take issue with any notion that the "knowledge of our faith" is built upon the historicity and inerrancy of the Bible. God's Word and the biblical text are not always synonymous, and faith is not limited to blind allegiance to a canonized text. I contend that responsible

---

13 Richards, E. Randolph, O'Brien, Brandon J., Misreading Scripture with Western Eyes: Removing Cultural Barriers to Better Understand the Bible (Downers Grove: Intervarsity Press, 2012)

Christian theology depends upon seven irreplaceable sources as repositories of faith: *1) Revelation, 2) the Human experience, 3) Scripture, 4)Tradition 5)Culture 6) Context, and 7) Reason.* Limiting faith to any concept of biblical historicity and inerrancy is not only wrong, but woefully irresponsible when ministering to people whose lives are chronically oppressed by biblically sanctioned ideologies. Unchallenged theology always leads to oppressive sociology.

Nevertheless, notwithstanding what my doctoral mentor, the late Dr. Samuel Dewitt Proctor, would assert, how we view the so-called Creation Story matters. The Creation Story profoundly shapes our view of the Redemption Story. The Creation Story matters to those who are serious about discovering creative ways to teach and preach the biblical text in ways that challenge, convict, and contend with obvious social evil. It matters to anyone interested in the redemptive possibilities gained from a liberating reading of the Creation Story. Scholars have long held that "Yahweh's power as Creator is the basis of the proclamation that he is the Redeemer."[14] The Creator God is also the Redeemer God, who redeems creation to live out the Creator's intent.

> The Creation Story matters to those who are serious about discovering creative ways to teach and preach the biblical text in ways that challenge, convict, and contend with obvious social evil.

---

14. Anderson, *Understanding the Old Testament,* (Englewood Cliffs: Princeton Hall, Inc., 1975) p. 7.

After centuries of hearing preaching and receiving the teaching of the traditional perspective of the Creation Story, I suspect a hermeneutical chokehold has been placed on African-American Christians. This hermeneutical chokehold limits the capacity of many preachers and teachers to responsibly interpret the biblical text in ways that consistently inspire the redemptive processes of liberatory praxis. The literal understanding of the Creation as cosmogony, as an accurate depiction of the creation of heaven and earth, is embedded in the biblical worldview of many perspectives.

The eminent Old Testament scholar Brevard Childs notes that, "Faith in creation is neither the basis nor the goal of the declarations in Gen., chs. 1 and 2. Rather, the position of both the Yahwist and the Priestly document is basically faith in salvation and election." In light of the salvation intent, I want to nudge us to consider an alternate possibility. I want to offer a liberatory Creation Story primer as an alternative to the dominant perspectives. I offer this perspective with full knowledge that it faces a head wind of biblical and theological resistance, none more obstinate than the faith perspective within the African-American community itself. Yet, it is offered as an alternative expression of hermeneutical resistance to the dominant, or in the words of the late Walter Wink, the "dominating powers."[15]

---

15. Wink, Walter, *Naming the Powers*, (Philadelphia: Fortress Press, 1984) Wink refers to the "Domination System" as a entire network of powers integrated around idolatrous values."

I share my humble contribution to the resistance movement against the dominating ideologies of Christian tradition. Just as a much-maligned professional quarterback risked a promising football career by taking a knee during the National Anthem as a protest against police brutality, I am, in fact, "taking a hermeneutical knee" for the millions across the centuries who have been theologically wounded by the religion of the empire and its imperialistic ideologies. I unapologetically assert that the following treatment of the Creation Story represents a form of hermeneutical resistance that I believe is consistent with the resistance movement of those who first compiled, shared, and liturgically experienced and expressed it. I am acutely aware that the interpretation offered breaks with the commonly held beliefs about the Creation Story, but I am convinced it is more consistent with the original intention than the one commonly held. Hopefully, what I offer is somehow considered as a viable possibility for hearing the text in a different way.

Virginia Hamilton gifts and enriches our understanding of Creation stories in her illustrated work, *In the Beginning: Creation Stories from Around the World*. Hamilton notes, "Creation myths describe a place and a time impossible for us to see for ourselves. People everywhere have creation myths, revealing how they see themselves to themselves in ways that are movingly personal."[16] In an absolutely engrossing publication, she offers Creation stories, many that are much older than the Judea

---

16 Hamilton, Virginia, *In The Beginning: Creation Stories From Around the World*, (San Diego: Pennyroyal Press, Inc.,1988), p. xi

Christian Creation story. The twenty-five collected stories range from the fascinating "The Pea-Pod Man" to the familiar "In the Beginning: Let There be Light," including one entitled the "The Frost Giant: Imir the Creator." Her observance of the prophetic nature of Creation stories startles and intrigues me because, as she says, "Myth stories about creation are different, however. In a prophetic voice, they relate events that seem outside of time and even beyond time itself. Creation myths take place before the 'once upon a time' of fairy tales."[17]

Hamilton considers the two Creation stories present within Genesis 1 and 2, even noting the distinct names used for God within the respective stories: Yahweh and Eloim ("J" and "E" sources, respectively). As it relates to Genesis 1, the Creation Story that concerns this writing, she wisely states, "The one-god concept is the main religious form in both Judaism and Christianity. Having one god means having one time and one world in which the heavenly Father is the supreme being. It is creation from the Word."[18] Bonhoeffer noted, "The only continuity between God and his word is the Word."

The Creation Story matters because the darkness, chaos, and emptiness so prevalent in our world demand a counter-narrative that possesses creative impetus. Accepting what is as what shall always be is not the faith posture of Bible-based faith. "Hu[man]ity has always suspected that behind all creation lies the abyss

---

17 Ibid., p. x
18 Op. cite, Sanders p.

of formlessness; that all creation is always ready to sink into the abyss of the formless; that the chaos, therefore, signifies the threat to everything created."[19] The Western Church in general, and the Black Church in particular, need to hear afresh, "Any one in Christ is a new creation. The old passes away. Behold, all things have become new."[20] New Creation faith must include new ways of hearing old stories.

Such a perspective is critical to biblical interpretation because of the Bible's acknowledgment of what Wes-Howard Brook call two religions "each pulling on people in opposite directions…one of the religions to be grounded in the experience of an ongoing relationship with the Creator God, leading to a covenant bond between God and God's people for the blessing and abundance of all people and all creation. The other, while sometimes claiming to be grounded in that same God, is actually a human invention used to justify and legitimate attitudes and behaviors that provide blessing and abundance for some at the expense of others."[21]

The context of the Creation Story makes it matter the more in a time when so much of what the Bible gives witness to is reflected in our world today. Insight into the Creation Story is provided in the cadence of each day being marked with "the evening and the morning." It is to this liberatingly enriching phrase that we now turn.

---

19 Childs.
20 2 Corinthians 5:17
21 Brook, Wes-Howard, "Come Out My People!" God's Call out of Empire in the Bible and Beyond, (Maryknoll, NY: Orbis Books, 2011), p.7.

DISCUSSION MATTERS

I contend that the opening story of the Bible sets the stage for how the Bible has been esteemed and interpreted on the one hand, or literally consumed and hermeneutically distorted on the other.

1. What have been your thoughts of the Creation Story?

2. Do you believe the Creation Story is an accurate depiction of the beginning of life on earth? Why?

3. I contend that responsible Christian theology depends upon seven irreplaceable sources as repositories of faith: *1) Revelation, 2) the Human experience, 3) Scripture, 4) Tradition 5) Culture 6) Context, and 7) Reason.*

4. What are the sources that you use to shape your understanding of the Christian faith?

5. Why has it been so easy for us to ignore findings of responsible biblical scholarship?

6. Brevard Childs makes the following observation, "Faith in creation is neither the basis nor the goal of the declarations in Gen., chs. 1 and 2. Rather, the position of both the Yahwist and the Priestly document is basically faith in salvation and election."

7. What changes for you if you considered salvation and faith as the goal of the Creation Story and not from the goal of faith in creation?

8. What changes for you if, in fact, the Creation Story is influenced by the Babylonian Exile and the Enuma Elish myth?

9. Scholars have long held that "Yahweh's power as Creator is the basis of the proclamation that he is the Redeemer."[22] How do we connect the Creation Story with the Redemption Story?

10. What does it mean to you that there are numerous Creation Stories in the world, many of which pre-date the Creation Story within the Judea-Christian tradition?

---

22 Anderson, *Understanding the Old Testament*, (*Englewood Cliffs: Princeton Hall, Inc., 1975*) p. 7.

CHAPTER 3

THE EVENING AND THE MORNING MATTERS

Subtly buried within the Creation story is a liturgical cadence that each day is augmented with the hymnic refrain, "the evening and the morning." Considering the liberatory perspective of the Bible, there seems to be a liturgical attempt to respond to some dark and oppressive experience with a new-day hope to be realized in the metaphor of "morning." Of interest to us should be a desire to know, what is the evening challenge of each day in creation? Likewise, what is the morning hope being offered in the genius of the Creation Story? It is the answers to these questions that shape the hermeneutical query of this writing. I believe it's worth knowing the hermeneutical significance of the evening and the morning, as well as how it might inform and shape contemporary preaching and teaching. Hence is the hermeneutical lens by which I approach these brief musings over the Creation Story. I invite us to see that each day, as metaphors of re-creating a more hopeful worldview, presents an evening challenge and a morning hope. Each day opens up with a death-dealing challenge to life and ends with a life-affirming hope for new life. Each day acknowledges the potential for great despair, but concludes buoyed by the creative power of a creative God that voices a hopeful morning. Each day addresses some oppressive expression of the dominant culture, but ends with the liberating impetus of the Creator God.

As I pore over each of the designated days of the Creation Story, I am drawn by the peculiar literary expression that sets the cadence of each day, the evening and the morning. The evening and the morning is more than the summary statement of a particular day. I assert that the evening and the morning represents a benedictory cadence of hopeful resistance. It seems that a people of faith brought into their worship space a story of creation that resisted the evening, or the oppressive hegemony that had been imposed upon them. During a dark night of relentless oppression, they spoke resistance faith by acknowledging the evening and declaring the doxology of the morning.

> The evening and the morning represents a benedictory cadence of hopeful resistance.

Critical to the faith that counters dark and chaotic evenings was a God that speaks creative activity that radically distinguishes the morning from the evening. Without a doubt, the creative energy of God's Word provided new-day hope in the midst of evening realities.

In biblical folklore, the evening, or the night, always stood for a time of challenge, human limitation, threat, transition, and the chaos of oppression. Estelle Frankel, an amazing spiritual teacher in Jewish mysticism informs us that, "For Jews, time always begins at night. On the Jewish calendar, each new day begins with nightfall rather than daybreak."[23] She further asserts that, "the darkness of night is associated with the fragmented state known as exile – the state of being disconnected from one's true place."[24] Conversely, the morning served as a symbol of hope, joy, newness, and liberation. Consider Exodus 16, verses 6–9, where we encounter the evening-morning motif as pivotal to the liberation experience. "At evening you shall know that the Lord has brought you out of the land of Egypt." Babylonian bondage and Egyptian oppression had worn deep into the souls of the people. It had been a difficult and dangerous experience, but it is within the evening of dark moments where the knowledge of the Liberator God was transformatively comprehended.

The episode in Exodus 16 articulates a scene where a recently liberated people became anxious about the menu of freedom. They complained. They argued. They became contentious over how God was frugally sustaining them in freedom in comparison to the accustomed menu of oppression. Their minds and attitudes had become darkened with doubt and despair. Yet, it was within the challenge of an evening experience that God intervened with morning possibilities and new beginnings. Evening would be a going-out time. As painful and debilitating as the evening experience might be, from a faith perspective, it

---

23 Frankel, Estelle, *Sacred Therapy: Jewish Spiritual Teachings on Emotional Healing and Inner Wholeness*, (Boston, MA: Shambhala Publications, Inc., 2003), p. 18
24 Ibid., p. 19

serves as the set-up time for new beginnings. What a statement of hope! What God began, God began in the evening!

Outside of the Jewish Holocaust, no experience has been fraught with dark, dehumanizing, chaotic, and emptiness like the African American one. Systematizing a commercial network where human chattel was exchanged required a psycho-socio-spiritual disruption among the enslaved and the enslavers. Darkness has to come upon the socio-spiritual psyche of a people to justify human enslavement and the accompanying violence needed to uphold such a system. Something of demonic proportion must possess one human to dehumanize other humans on the level necessary to perpetuate the practices of human slavery as experienced in America. This disruption became so thorough that for hundreds of years blacks were born into the empty world of slavery and whites were born into the chaos of white supremacy. Black life has been one of perpetual darkness in America, compounded by the fear-filled antics of white people.

A recent visit to the National Museum of African American History in Washington, DC, and the Lynching Memorial in Montgomery, Alabama, allowed us graphic images, stories, and snapshots of how the darkness of slavery and the Jim Crow South savagely gripped this country. Acknowledging the evening represents the redemptive genius of our Jewish comrades in oppression, because it offered a context from which to aspire for the morning. James Weldon Johnson captured the experience when he poetically gave his Creation account from an African American perspective. He wrote:

> And far as the eye of God could see
> Darkness covered everything,
> Blacker than a hundred midnights
> Down in a cypress swamp.

When the knowledge of a creative God is experienced in the evening, the morning brings about an alternative experience. "And in the morning you shall see the glory of the Lord; for He hears your complaints against the Lord" (Exod. 16:6–9). The Exodus text illustrates and amplifies the metaphorical genius of Genesis 1. We are given liberatory proof that no expression of oppressive darkness, meaningless injustices, senseless violence, or chaotic inequities can resist the creative energy of a life-affirming God. Even when the enslaved, demeaned, and dehumanized collude with their own oppression, creative possibilities can still be birthed.

Leroi Jones (*Blues People*) and Howard Thurman (*The Negro Speaks of Life and Death*) presented amazing insight into the subtleties of black music. The blues (Jones) and the spirituals (Thurman) demonstrate the hermeneutical genius of our enslaved and oppressed ancestors. Of late, I have mused over the hermeneutical intent of some of the songs of my childhood, many of which are rarely sung in today's Black Church. What were those Negro bards really insinuating when inviting the Church to sing such songs as "There's Gonna Be A Great Gettin' up Morning"? What evening experience were they responding to when they sang, "My Lord Gettin' Us Ready for the Great Day"? I cannot conceive of the "Great Day" being exclusively grounded in heavenly hope. Having lived the black experience I doubt seriously if they were engaging in some psycho-spiritual defense in preparation for the sweet by-and-by. The "Great Day" had to have been an eschatological vision of a day freed of the dehumanizing entrapments of racial injustice and inequity. Much like the beloved Psalm 30, verse 5b, states, "Weeping may endure for a night, but joy comes in the morning," I believe embedded within the lyrics of those songs are Creation-like liturgical energies that offered up new-day possibilities.

In the spirit of our ancestors, both African and Jewish, I offer sermonic musings of what an evening and morning hermeneutic might look, read, and even sound like. Since preaching is what I do most, I believe preaching will reveal best this alternative perspective of the Creation Story. At best, you might be encouraged to further study the Creation Story. At worst, you will have given me opportunity to share with you some hermeneutical time. While I have tweaked the following expositions to assist in their readability and added a pre-word, each day was initially a sermon prepared and preached for the Black Church experience. Thus, I offer the following musings as hermeneutical primers for the consideration of new beginnings for people who need them.

DISCUSSION MATTERS

1. How do you define or interpret the liturgical cadence" the evening and the morning"?

2. How did you react to the to the invitation to consider each day as metaphors of re-creating a more hopeful worldview, by presenting an evening challenge and a morning hope?

3. Discuss the assertion that "the evening and the morning represent a benedictory cadence of hopeful resistance."

4. Can you identity some "evening" experiences in American experience?

5. Are there any "morning" experiences that you can identify?

6. How does connecting with the reality of a creative God serve to redefine the darkness of oppression?

7. Are there other songs within our culture that poignantly connect the tension of an evening of oppression and the hopefulness of the morning? Please cite.

CHAPTER 4

THE FIRST DAY
NEW BEGINNINGS FOR PEOPLE WHO NEED THEM

TEXT: *"In the beginning God created the heavens and the earth. The earth was without form, and void; and darkness was on the face of the deep. And the Spirit of God was hovering over the face of the waters. Then God said, "Let there be light"; and there was light. And God saw the light, that it was good; and God divided the light from the darkness. God called the light Day, and the darkness He called Night. So the evening and the morning were the first day" (Gen. 1:1–5, NKJV).*

The Pre-Word: The evening is a violently sustained worldview shrouded in the constructs of meaninglessness, emptiness, and darkness. "Blacker than a hundred midnights" poetically describes politically sustained oppression. The morning comes as divine intervention to counter the prevailing darkness. After over two generations of being exiled from the friendly and familiar, it became difficult to see any light within the exilic tunnel of despair. How do people get to light through such pronounced darkness?

People in struggle create ways of framing life in modalities that encourage and strengthen personal and communal resilience. Without the benefit of academic training, or familiarity with any particular school of thought, people have been known

> While in Babylonian exile, a struggling people grabbed this story and created for all time a liturgy of new beginnings for people who need them.

to develop memorable phrases that literally serve as liturgies for life. Such phrases as, "When life gives you lemons, make lemonade," has empowered people to live beyond sour situations. (The new take on that is, "When life gives you lemons, get the tequila, the salt" and make a Margarita). "When in hot water, make tea" has helped people through self-inflicted trouble. "You play the hand that has been dealt to you" has enabled people to creatively live their way out of life-imposed difficulties. Who of us hasn't used "every cloud has a silver lining" to help someone live through a dark day?

If you have heard, or ever used, any of these sayings, it should not be difficult for you to understand how people in struggle take what's available and develop liturgies for new beginnings. This is, in fact, what the Creation Story represents in the biblical text. It represents a struggling people's attempt to take what was before them and provide a liturgy for new beginnings.

While in Babylonian exile, a struggling people grabbed this story and created for all time a liturgy of new beginnings for people who need them. The intent was never to provide a scientific understanding of how the world, or the cosmos, was created. Nor was this an attempt to set Creationism against Evolution. The intent was to transform a lemon situation into lemonade of new beginning, or take the salt and lime and make a refreshing Margarita of visionary possibilities.

Don't hang up on me now! Please don't tune me out! I believe this Creation Story provides a powerful vision for new beginnings. I don't know about you, but most of the people I know, especially people of faith, could use the message of this text more than they need an argument about the text. If we allow this text to do what it's supposed to do, I believe its message could revolutionize some things in our lives. Interestingly, this text has been benignly sitting in the Bible all these years; but right now, it could energize us into life far more hopeful than we can imagine. Therefore, I want to open this adventure by proposing that hopeful living is the result of people's lives being energized for new beginnings through creative imagining.

As I survey my life, the times when I was most hopeful, most energized, imaginative, and most excited about life, were when my life was wrapped around an episode of new beginnings. A new toy as a boy, some new clothes as a teen, a new love as a man, a new child as a parent, a new grandbaby as a grandparent, a new job as a professional, a new ministry as a teacher/evangelist, a new idea as a preacher, a new member as a pastor, a new opportunity as a servant, a new place to visit as a traveler, a new book to read as a student, a new computer as a techie, a new dish to eat, a new wine to taste, a new house to experience, or a new song to sing. After thirty-plus years of serving churches that are historically slow to change, it still gladdens my heart when the Lord's people get excited about making the old gospel real in a new way.

While the Jews lingered long in exile and suffered long in Egypt, they realized that nothing damages a people more than the despair that things will never get better. What prompted the writing of this text was the fact they understood the psychological and spiritual damage done to a people who stop believing in new beginnings. I have read a lot of stories in my life and viewed thousands of movies and shows. What all of them have in common is the opening line or an opening scene that suggests, "Once upon a time." When we examine the phrase under the hermeneutical microscope of Genesis 1, a disturbing reality is seen. Once upon a time suggest that beginnings happen only once within a framework of time. Once upon a time is not a biblical construct. Once upon a time is not a faith perspective. Once upon a time is the prelude to an oppressive narrative that usually concludes with "The End." Once upon a time is the construct of those who believe that everything that happens in life will happen only once. Once upon a time is an oppressive perspective that distorts life.

However, the people who penned the words of our text developed a faith perspective that informed them that what God has done once, God can do again! God might not do it the same way, but God is always doing the same thing—seeking to save, to heal, to deliver, to redeem, to liberate, and to transform. They knew of a God who delivered them from Egypt, delivered them from the dens of Assyrian exile, and would deliver them from the fiery furnace of Babylonian exile.

The other day, while having my car washed, someone came in with a Hyundai Genesis. Genesis is not a car! Genesis was not made in Korea. Genesis actually comes from the word *bereshith*, which speaks of beginnings, many beginnings. In the language of the biblical text, we don't live once upon a time, we live in the fullness of time, and in the fullness of time there are multiple opportunities for new beginnings.

Perhaps a visit from Nicodemus would help us. He would tell us how confused he was when Jesus told him about a new beginning when he said, "You must be born again." Maybe Paul can intrude in this conversation and remind us, "If any one be in Christ, he is a new creature. Old things pass away. Behold, all things have become new." Isaiah would add to our query by reminding us that God is always about doing a new thing.

The year 2018 had to have been one of the craziest years in our lives. We saw things we never saw before, and folks were doing things we thought we would never see again. So many approached 2019 with dread, fearing the madness that the age of Trump might continue to bring. Yet, the opening words of the book we hold dear provide clues for us that come what may we are people of new beginnings. I want to explore this ancient text and glean from it a few helpful truths on new beginnings, because we need it.

When we listen to these ancient bards speaking from the bowels of an oppressive world, they inform us that new beginnings happen when people prioritize God. It's in the text! The whole Bible begins on these words, *"In the beginning God,"* or *"Bereshith Elohim."* The prioritizing of God provides the opening for new beginnings. If anything new is going to happen, God must be first and foremost.

For the people who wrote this text, the prioritizing of God minimized the impact any other power or system tried to have on their lives. Zora Neale Hurston wrote poignantly of how a community devastated by a hurricane walked, "broken with ignorance and ugly with poverty," yet they gazed into the darkness and "their eyes were watching God."[25] My beloved Jewish brother, Dr. Michael Lerner, profoundly articulates hope for the prioritizing of God in his incredible book Jewish Renewal. Lerner opines:

"The ultimate Force governing the world, the Force that has created the entirety of Being, is the energy that presses for transcendence toward a world in which all Being manifests its fullest ethical and spiritual potential, a world in which human beings recognize one another both in our particularity and in our ability to manifest ethical and spiritual possibility."[26]

Too many of us have limited our new-beginning possibilities because we have allowed the darkness to limit God, and

---

25 Hurston, Zora Neale, *Their Eyes Were Watching God*, J. B. Lippincot & Co, 1937
26 Lerner, Michael, *Jewish Renewal: Path to Healing and Transformation*, (New York, NY, Putnam Book, 1994) p. 65.

in some instances to eclipse God. A God limited by darkness can never be prioritized. Thus, there's a need among us to stare into the darkness and still see God. Unfortunately, we have constructed darkness options. We have too many options before we consider God. We consult too many other sources, especially the splitting nuances of our own troubled personalities. Likewise, too many of us limit our new beginnings because we have given the darkness of evil too much power. We have allowed the craziness of the media, the maddening drams of Trump's Washington, and the seduction of the market to rob us of new-beginning possibilities.

Since the text begins with God, something needs to be said about religion. Religion is not God, and too often, religion gets in the way of God. If there is any area where we need a new beginning, it's in the area of religion. Religion, especially that espoused by oppressors, gets in the way of new beginnings because religion gets stuck in the past. Too many of us are still yearning for "old-time religion," and too many preachers are preaching old to old folks in an old church doing church the old way. We have become parrots, repeating only what we have heard rather than a word of new beginnings.

God is not a God of the past, but a God of the now and the yet to come. Perhaps one of the most powerful things that happen when we prioritize God is not just the minimizing of evil powers and impotent religion, but prioritizing God puts us in our right place. The reason we have so many psalms that lift up God and put us in our place is that we tend to think we are running things. The psalms serve to remind us that life begins with God, not with us. "The earth is the Lord's and the fullness thereof, and they who dwell therein."[27] "What is man, that you are mindful of Him. You created him lower than the angels."[28] "Know that the Lord, he is God. It is He who has made us, and not we ourselves. We are his people and the sheep of his pasture."[29]

Whenever we are serious about new beginnings, we must prioritize God. Secondly, the text helps us to see that new beginnings happen when people get honest about their empty and chaotic lives. It's in the text! "The earth was without form, and void; and darkness was on the face of the deep." From the perspective of exile, in the belly of oppression, the people became brutally honest about their life situations. They set to liturgy and song that a diminished perspective of God emptied life of form and darkened life with despair.

Too often, we can't get to our new beginnings because we are not honest about the chaotic emptiness of our lives. We have found sophisticated ways to deny that we have made a mess out of our lives. We can never experience the separation of light from darkness without first acknowledging the darkness. The other day, I listened as a young man blamed Adam and Eve for the mess in his life. He blamed Adam and Eve for his parents' cruelty and his own painful antics. Adam and Eve hav-

---

27 Psalm 24:1
28 Psalm 8:4
29 Psalm 100:3

en't messed up our lives. We've messed up our own lives! When blacks were rarely seen on television, we had *The Flip Wilson Show*. Flip Wilson used to say that the devil made him do all the things that messed up his life. Adam and Eve had as much to do with destroying our family relations, emptying our bank accounts, and putting our children on drugs as Flip Wilson's devil. *You* wrecked your family. *You* messed up your money! *You* jacked up your life! *You* put yourself in all the places without form, darkness, void, and chaotic. While the systems and structures of oppression conspire to perpetuate chaotic emptiness, we contribute to its power and maintenance.

We must be honest about the fact that whatever is going on in our lives, we had something to do with it. I weary of people who come to church and pretend that their life is blessed when the whole world, especially their family, knows better. The reason I come to church is because I need to be in church. I don't have anything better to do than to expose my wearied soul to the life-giving power of worship and Word. I need to be in church so I can put myself in position for God to do what God does next in the text. The text says, "And the Spirit of God was hovering over the face of the water." New beginnings happen when people position themselves for a spiritual experience. I'm glad to hear God is blessing people's lives, but I also know that the only reason God is blessing is because the Spirit of God had to hover over some dark and chaotic mess and bring about an illuminating spiritual experience.

Years ago, I heard Dr. Charles G. Adams of the Hartford Street Baptist Church, Detroit, Michigan, exegete this text. Dr. Adams said the word used for hover is a sexual term. It was used to describe the anxious and animal-like trembling to mate, or to copulate. The Spirit of God was moving back and forth, waiting for a chance to create something different. God's Spirit was anxious about bringing into reality a new life that could never happen without God getting involved. With all of the darkness in our world, and even in our lives, God is hovering, anxiously wanting to birth a new beginning.

Some of us have been keeping God at bay, pushing God away from doing what only God can do. We have been rejecting God either out of a construct of self-reliance, or a belief in technology-based relief. If we really want God to birth new beginnings in our lives, we must yield to the Spirit. When we yield to the Spirit of God, we can better hear the word of God; and I bring you to the final point of this opening word on new beginnings.

New beginnings happen when people receive God's Word as light for a new day. The text says, "Then God said, 'Let there be light'; and there was light." "Then God said." God doesn't say anything until the chaotic emptiness and the nagging darkness is acknowledged. A new day doesn't come until after the darkness is acknowledged and there is a need to divide, or separate, light from the darkness. New beginnings can only happen when God speaks a word that gives us light for a new day.

For years, I have tried to teach this text. I struggled to get the Lord's people to see that the light spoken of in verses 3–5 is not physical light. Physical light, such as the sun, moon, and stars, are not mentioned until verse 14. The light spoken of in our text is the light of comprehensive understanding. Light must first happen in our minds before it can ever happen in our world. We succumb to the darkness until light breaks forth in our conscious. Ironically, we don't know darkness from light until God separates the two. Notice in verse 2. The world situation was characterized as "darkness on the face of the deep." The socio-politico, psycho-spiritual were noted as "darkness on the face of the deep. " In verse 4, God uses light to divide the light from the darkness.

New beginnings must first happen in our minds before they can ever happen in our world. I pray someone gets this! I pray someone who needs a new beginning will understand that the world becomes brighter when the mind becomes brighter. John used this same story to talk about Jesus. John would later testify about Jesus. He would say, "In Him was life, and the life was the light of men. And the light shines in the darkness, and the darkness did not comprehend it."[30] "The Word became flesh and dwelt among us, and we beheld his glory . . ."[31]

I can't speak for anyone else, but I need new beginnings in my life. I need the joy that new beginnings bring. I need the hope that a new beginning births. I need the energy that only a

---

30 John 1:4
31 John 1:14

new beginning can fuel. Therefore, I made up my mind that I'm going to trust God's Word to give me light for a new day.

Can I tell the truth? I don't know what this year is going to bring, but whatever it brings, I'm living for a new beginning. I believe God's Word, that "in the beginning God." People can talk about "make America great again," but I believe God can create a new America for all people. People can advocate building walls that separate, but I believe in a God who can unite the disunited. I believe God can take the darkness of this present American mess and bring forth new life. I believe God can create a new America "where justice rolls down like waters and righteousness as a mighty stream."[32]

No wonder our spiritual ancestors would never leave a Christmas, or a Watchnight Service, without singing:

> **Walk in the light, beautiful light,**
> **Come where the dewdrops of mercy shine bright.**
> **Oh shine all around us by day and by night,**
> **Jesus is, Jesus is the light of the world.**

"And the evening and the morning was the first day." The evening of this day is the darkness, chaos, and emptiness of an oppressive construct pervading life with a litany of falsehoods. It's evening when the most respected office in the world has been darkened by corruption and a constant barrage of lies. It's evening when the minds of the masses have been shrouded

---

[32] Amos 5:24

with untruths, often disguised in patriotism, religion, nature, or some distorted notion of manifest destiny. The evening is a world darkened by white supremacy, emptied by black inferiority, and chaotically jumbled in impersonal materialism.

The evening represents the night of an oppressive experience and perspective, and the morning happens when light is distinguished from such. The evening is a nation pledged to white privilege and black denial. The morning breaks forth when the protestations of the oppressed are incarnated in marching feet and economic boycotts. The evening is the abuse and silencing of half the nation on the basis of gender inequality. The morning comes when feminists and womanists voices refuse to be silent and join in a chorus of #MeToo! The evening is the painful legacy of immigrant exploitation. The morning comes when immigrants organize and assert their humanity. The evening is a nation committed to imperialism. The morning comes when democracy becomes more than political jargon, but a moral responsibility to be lived out in faith.

Yes, the morning is the outbreak of truth that sets people free to reimagine the world in a new way. The morning is a new vision, a vision that separates light from darkness. Thank God

> The evening is a nation pledged to white privilege and black denial. The morning breaks forth when the protestations of the oppressed are incarnated in marching feet and economic boycotts.

for Jesus! Jesus separated the light from the darkness when he declared, "I am the Light of the world."[33]

DISCUSSION MATTERS

1. Do you agree with the assertion that "people in struggle create ways of framing life in modalities that encourage and strengthen personal and communal resilience"?

2. Are you familiar with the terms Creationism and Evolutionism? If so, what position do you generally lean toward?

3. Discuss the proposition that" hopeful living is the result of people's lives being energized for new beginnings through creative imagining."

4. How have you reacted to experiencing something new in life?

5. What are your thoughts on religion? Do you believe religion functions best when facilitating new beginnings?

6. What would happen in your life if you prioritized God?

7. Can you identify some ways in which oppression empties life of meaning?

---

[33] John 8:12

8. What are some of the expressions of darkness prevalent in our world today?

9. Please react to the assertion that "light must first happen in our minds before it can ever happen in our world."

10. Are there ways in which our minds darken our perspective of the world? How so?

11. What is the evening of the first day? The morning?

12. How do such "evening" and "morning" perspectives manifest themselves in our world

CHAPTER 5

THE SECOND DAY:
FAITH IN THE FIRMAMENT

TEXT: *"Then God said, 'Let there be a firmament in the midst of the waters, and let it divide the waters from the waters.' Thus God made the firmament, and divided the waters which were under the firmament from the waters which were above the firmament; and it was so. And God called the firmament Heaven. So the evening and the morning were the second day" (Gen. 1:6–8).*

A Pre-Word: The evening is a world defined by uncontrollable forces that intimidate and domesticate. It is a world where people feel as if they have no control over their lives, and their destiny has been determined. It is a state of being that denies faith as a viable option, and where life is dominated by fear. However, the morning comes when faith in the Unseen becomes more powerful than fear of the seen. When we live by faith, we exorcise ourselves from the dominating spirits of uncontrollable fear of unimaginable expressions of evil. How then do we maintain faith when overwhelmed by the uncontrollable?

Indiana Jones was a movie series in which Harrison Ford starred as a daring archeologist. As an archeologist, Indiana Jones used the science of archeology to seek and examine the cultural relics of people and civilizations that no longer existed. He made archeology fun, because there was always some dark power to overcome. The intrigue of the movie series was the ominous presence of some evil force that wanted to keep the present from experiencing the treasures of the past.

One Sunday, the *San Francisco Chronicle* presented a powerful article depicting the declining state of the Black Church in Oakland, as well as in San Francisco. As usual, Richmond churches were not mentioned in the writing, but the article noted what we all know to be true. The Black Church, throughout the Bay Area, is at risk of becoming a cultural relic. The ageing-out of most of our congregations and the lack of interest and commitment of the younger generation have set us on a course of congregational extinction. This is nothing new. It's nobody's fault. Things have just changed! Pastor Newman stated over twenty years ago, "Our churches need to consider merging, or we will go out of business." Perhaps the Black Church may be in the best position it has been in a very long time. We are being forced to consider the God of New Life in the midst of uncontrollable circumstances.

Before we lock the doors, perhaps we need a few black biblical and Christian archeologists who will help us better understand what brought us to this place, and how we might experience new beginnings. What today's text provides is a perspective on new beginnings for people who need them. I must confess, and apologize if necessary, that this interpretation will not be the one we got from our parents and grandparents. I'm going to invite you to join me in an adventure to hear the story as the people who wrote heard it. Therefore, I propose that for us to experience a new beginning, we must have faith in the firmament.

Most of us grew up on nursery rhymes. We learned how to sing doing nursery rhymes. We learned how to talk on nursery rhymes. Some of us were put to sleep with the soothing singing of nursery rhymes. Yet, if our parents and teachers knew the backstories of those nursery rhymes, they would never have used them, and we never would have gone to sleep on nursery rhymes. In fact, the backstories would have given us nightmares. Consider:

> Baa, baa, black sheep, have you any wool?
> Yes sir, yes sir, three bags full!
> One for the master, one for the dame,
> And one for the little boy who cries down the lane.

The backstory to that nursery rhyme was a protest against a harsh wool tax in England. One-third went to the king/empire, and one-third was for the Church, leaving the farmer crying that he only had one-third of the product that he worked hard for. It was a protest against economic inequity. Consider further:

> Rub-a-dub dub, three men in a tub, three men in a tub,
> And who do you think they are? The butcher, the baker, the candlestick
> Maker, And all of them gone to the fair.

The backstory to that nursery rhyme was that it was not three men in the tubs, it was three maids in the tub, who were involved in scandalous relations with respectable men—the butcher, the baker, and the candlestick maker, and it was all going down at the local fair. It was an exposé on political corruption. You all still didn't get it. Consider also:

> Ten little, nine little, eight little Indians,
> Seven little, six little, five little Indians,
> Four little, three little, two little Indians,
> One little Indian boy, and then there was none.

The backstory to this one should be obvious. You start with ten Indians—and in some renditions, it was ten niggers—and you end up with none. It was describing the violent and systematic extermination of the Native Americans, and was even used to slur black people coming out of slavery.

The backstory to the Creation narrative is a people at risk of being spiritually and psychologically exterminated by the violent intrusions of Babylonian exile.

The backstory to the Creation narrative is a people at risk of being spiritually and psychologically exterminated by the violent intrusions of Babylonian exile. As depicted in Jeremiah, Daniel, Isaiah, and others, the brutal intrusions of Babylonian exile placed them at risk of losing a sense of who they were. Thus, they grabbed the available materials of their oppressors and transformed them into stories of new beginnings. As they listened to the false claims of their oppressor, they creatively reshaped an ancient story so that when the oppressor listened, he heard one thing, but when they sang, it meant something else. This story is actually older than the Bible, older than the Jewish nation; but it was a tool used to re-imagine new beginnings.

It was like when our barefooted slave ancestors joined in singing, "You got shoes, I got shoes, all of God's chillen got shoes." The slave master heard one thing, but we were saying something else. When we sang, "Steal Away," the overseer heard one thing, but we were saying something else. When we sang, "On Jordan Stormy Banks I Stand," the white preacher heard one thing, but we were saying something else. In the midst of the violent and brutal intrusions upon their humanity, Nebuchadnezzar and the keepers of the Babylonian Empire heard one thing, but the marginalized Jews were saying something else.

Like Indiana Jones, the research has been done, and I know dark forces don't want to bless our lives with the treasures of the past. There are dark forces that don't want you to hear the truth of what I am presenting, because the truth might set you free from the religion of the oppressor. Yet, the truth of this story is not a focus on the Creation, but a focus on the Creator. Creation is a verb. Creator is a noun. God is the subject. Two words begin this story by making a grand announcement about the leading subject, but it takes four of our words to twist its intent and focus on verbs. "Bereshith Elohim," "In the beginning God," accurately interpreted, "When God begins."

In the previous chapter, I shared with you that the people who penned the words of our text developed a faith perspective that informed them that what God had done once, God can do it again. God might not do it the same way, but God is always doing the same thing—seeking to save, to heal, to deliver, to redeem, to liberate, and to transform. The people of our text knew of a God who delivered them from Egypt, delivered them from the dens of Assyrian exile, and would deliver them from the fiery furnace of Babylonian exile. For God to create, the dark emptiness of oppression had to be acknowledged. "The earth was without form, and void; and darkness was on the face of the deep."[34]

As we look at America and listen to the noise, it's time for some new-beginning people to announce that the world is without form, and void, and darkness is all over it. We need an announcement that this American dream is a nightmare, and all the Washingtonian lies have left us empty, void, and full of darkness. We need an announcement that the Creator has determined that we need order, and the first order of new beginnings is, "Let there be light."

Let there first be the light of comprehensive understanding. We need our minds delivered from the oppressive constructs of the enemy. We need the light of a liberating life perspective to emerge out of this American darkness, and grant us illuminating insight. Let a light go on in our minds that will light up our world and separate what we know is night from day, and what is

---

34 Genesis 1:2

day from the night. And the Bible said, "So the evening and the morning were the first day."

On the second day, the Bible says, "Then God said, 'Let there be a firmament in the midst of the waters, and let it divide the waters from the waters.'"[35] The backstory to the second day was a response to the reality cited in verse 2. Verse 2 illustrated what was said in verse 1, that "the earth was without form and void; and darkness was on the face of the deep." The backstory was an understanding that the waters represented the uncontrollable. Water can be of great use, but left to its own devices, water can destroy. Water has tremendous potential, but it was understood to be essentially uncontrollable. Water was the primary element of the chaos, and we know water lacks form. It's well-known that water seeks its own level."

The people who wrote this text believed that the waters symbolized the uncontrollable. The evening is life deluged with the uncontrollable. It shows up when we do things we know are not in our best interest, but we do them anyway. We are living in the waters! How many of you have found yourselves in situations that you knew would not serve you well? After all of these years, some of us old folks still have uncontrollable urges and are too weak to withstand certain realities, because we've lived too long in contexts of the uncontrollable. We live in the waters when we subject ourselves to forces that don't mean us any good; none more deadly than senseless violence. Paul

---

35 Genesis 1:6

described our living in the waters tendencies when he said, "The evil I don't want to do I find myself doing." Water is not useful until it has been brought under control, and the only one who controls the waters is God.

Across the years, we've heard sermons and lessons promoting the idea that God took nothing and made something. The Bible doesn't say that! The Bible says, "The earth was without form, and void; and darkness was on the face of the deep. And the Spirit of God was hovering over the waters." God took that which was available. God took that which lacked form, void, and[36] operating in the realm of the uncontrollable and spoke words of new beginnings. God said, "Let there be a firmament."[37] Let there be a realm of existence that puts space between the uncontrollable." And the only thing that can put space between the uncontrollable is a firm faith perspective.

The ancients of this text understood that this new beginning, or new creation provided by the Creator, was that there was the earth filled with water, uncontrollable, and between the uncontrollable was a firmament that separated the uncontrollable from the uncontrollable. The only thing that separates, or keeps, the uncontrollable waters below the earth and the uncontrollable waters above the earth was a dome, or the firmament. Verse 8 says, ***"And God called the firmament Heaven."*** The Hebrew word for firmament is *raqia*. The word is used only 17 times in the Bible, including the Psalms. In Ezekiel, an

---

[36] Genesis 1:1
[37] Genesis 1:3

exilic prophet, the firmament appears five times, and only once in Daniel. God created the firmament, and then God called the firmament "heaven." Bishop Sean Teal would say, "He determined the firmament. He declared the firmament, and God defined the firmament."

Heaven was not a pie-in-the-sky construct; that's a construct of the oppressor. Our oppressors understood that a reality away from here is the enticement offered when living here is too painful because of the pervasiveness of the uncontrollable. Yet, heaven in this text represented a firm space in life, a raqia that allowed people to live in the midst of the uncontrollable. It's in the text! "Let there be a firmament in the midst of the waters . . ."[38] People who need new beginnings understand that new beginnings happen in the midst of the chaos.

New beginnings happen even when we live among so much that we can't control, but have faith in One who has control. New beginnings emerge from the craziness of the uncontrollable. New beginnings happen when people walk by faith and not by sight. That's what we hear in Psalm 150, "Praise the Lord! Praise God in his sanctuary. Praise Him in his mighty firmament."[39] New beginnings are what we hear in Hebrews 11, "Now faith is the substance of things hoped for, the evidence of things not seen. For by it the elders obtained a good report/testimony. By faith we understand the worlds were framed by

---

38 Genesis 1:6
39 Psalm 150:1

the word of God, so that things which are seen were not made of things which are visible."[40]

New beginnings happen when people live by faith that no matter what craziness we might be experiencing in the waters, there is a firmament. There is a firm place where we can put our faith. There is a reality in the midst of the waters that we can firmly cling to, and for us our firmament, our raqia, is Jesus. You all know the story. The disciples would testify that in an uncontrollable situation, the waters from above and waters below, Jesus showed up walking on the water. Jesus spoke and the waters behaved. Jesus became a firmament in the midst of the waters. Our faith in him is our firmament, our raqia, and that's why we sing:

> Our hope is built on nothing less, than Jesus's blood and righteousness.
> I dare not trust a sweetest frame, but wholly lean on Jesus' name.
> On Christ, the solid rock I stand, all other ground is sinking sand.
> All other ground is sinking sand.

The evening and the morning is the second day. The evening is non-faith, or doubt; the morning is faith. We dare not trust the sweetest frame, but wholly lean on Jesus's name.

---

[40] Hebrews 11:1-3

DISCUSSION MATTERS

1. What were your thoughts on the "backstories" of the nursery rhymes?

2. Are there other interesting "backstories" that you know of?

3. What about the "backstory" proposed in this writing on the Creation Story?

4. Does the "backstory" in the Creation story seem valid? If not, why not?

5. What are your thoughts on the assertion the writers of the Creation Story "reshaped an ancient story so that when the oppressor listened, he heard one thing, but when they sang, it meant something else."

6. Enslaved Africans made cultural art of saying, or singing one thing, but meaning something else. The technical word for this practice is "circumvent." Are there any current practices where oppressed people are engaging in circumvent? How so?

7. What are your thoughts on the perspective of the "firmament'?

8. Are there instances where we are being challenged to live a life of faith in the midst of uncontrollable forces? If so, how so?

CHAPTER 6

THE THIRD DAY:
THE LET-BE GOD IN A MAKE-BE WORLD

TEXT: *"Then God said, 'Let the waters under the heavens be gathered together into one place, and let the dry land appear'; and it was so. 1And God called the dry land Earth, and the gathering together of the waters He called Seas. And God saw that it was good. Then God said, 'Let the earth bring forth grass, the herb that yields seed, and the fruit tree that yields fruit according to its kind, whose seed is in itself, on the earth'; and it was so. And the earth brought forth grass, the herb that yields seed according to its kind, and the tree that yields fruit, whose seed is in itself according to its kind. And God saw that it was good. So the evening and the morning were the third day" (Gen. 1:9–13).*

A Pre-Word: The evening of the text is a surrendering of the human spirit to the dehumanizing definitions of oppression in all of its demonic expressions. When human beings allow themselves to be defined by a spiritually alien construct, we start doing things alien to our divine makeup. Moreover, when forced to comply with constructs that separate us from our true selves, we set in perpetuity the procreation of our own oppression. The morning, however, is the acknowledgement of a God that calls forth creation to be what it was created to be. When homo sapiens grasp the intention of God for all creation, it liberates us to join in the cadence of a let-be God. How then do we grasp the reality of a let-be God?

In Bermuda, Louisiana, there's a plantation called the Oakland Plantation. It is the plantation where my late father was born. Eerie, for me, because I was born in Oakland, California. On the Oakland Plantation is a decaying building that once housed a school where my father attended. Across the street from that school is another building that housed a school that my father was never permitted to enter, let alone attend. The Saint Matthew's school went up to the eighth grade, while the school across the street went up to the twelfth grade; both schools funded and regulated by the United States government. White children received a twelfth-grade education, while black people could only go to the eighth grade.

As the child of sharecroppers, two generations removed from slavery, it was largely understood that black people existed for one reason only: to work for white people. Daddy wanted to go to school, but the grueling demands of the cotton field, and the cruel expectations of the Jim Crow South, required that he work. I suspect that the reason my parents believed so much in work was because the world in which they were born was defined by work.

However, on that same plantation was a church, the New Nazarene Missionary Baptist Church. While the demands of the plantation deprived him of a quality education, the spiritual ethos of the church provided him a space where he could cultivate a relationship with an all-loving God. The relationship

Daddy had with an all-loving God gave him hope to imagine life beyond the plantation. While his education was limited, his theology was without limits. While he lived in a world that didn't think much of him, what he thought about God inspired him to believe that life was not a dead-end, limited by the dehumanizing constructs of Jim Crow, but a journey of new beginnings. In a world defined by Jim Crow, plantation-born sharecroppers needed new beginnings.

For over thirty years I have been trying to do what my grandfather did, who served as pastor of that plantation church, which is to help the descendants of slaves and sharecroppers expand their theology. I am clear that my role as pastor and preacher is primarily a local church theologian. I engage in what the people of our text were doing, which is to expand our talk about God in ways that impact how we live in the world. I am not a scientist, nor is the Bible a science book. I'm not a biologist, nor is the Bible a biology book. I'm not a mathematician, nor is the Bible a mathematics book. I'm not an economist, nor is the Bible an economics book. While I might have a historical perspective, the Bible is not a history book. The Bible is a book composed of a people's theology, much of it penned in the poetic language of liturgy. It is their engagement in "God talk" that inspired their beliefs in new beginnings, even in a world that sought to define and limit them.

I believe it helpful for us that whenever we open the Bible, we understand that it's not about science, biology, math, or history, it's about God. Our time in this text will be helpful to us all if we would agree that preaching at its best is God-talk that helps people imagine new beginnings. Preaching ought to help people see beyond where they are and imagine where God wants them to be. Again, Genesis is not a scientific theory, nor an economic one. It is not a biological presentation, nor a historical perspective. It is a book composed of the witness of a people who needed new beginnings.

When you get time, research or Google Enuma Elish, or the Babylonian creation stories. The Babylonian creation stories provided a story that shaped the policies and worldview of Babylon. The Enuma Elish is a violent story, where gods kill gods, children gods kill mother gods, and human beings are created from the blood of one god to be servants to the gods. Babylon, which literally means "gates of the gods," became the place where human beings were subject to other human beings.

The idea was to keep people within the gates of Babylon, where people were made to do what others wanted them to do. Babylon was the place where the best and the brightest were violently coerced into believing what the Babylonians wanted them to believe; made to do what the Babylonians wanted them to do; to talk the way the Babylonians wanted them to talk, and to live the way the Babylonians wanted them to live. Babylon, like America, seduced people into believing that it was the greatest and most powerful country in the world.

Babylon is the prototype of empire. Babylon represents evil powers in high places. It is where people are made to be what the Babylonians wanted them to be. It's a make-be world. It's where people were made to do what the empire needed done, made to live the way the empire wanted them to live, and even to worship the way the empire wanted them to worship. Babylon represented the central challenge to biblical faith. It was a make-be world supported by make-be gods.

> The most dominant character in the story is God, and the most creative words in the story are God's words, "Let there be."

The text of this chapter invites us to consider the incredibly liberating reality of life being shaped by a let-be God. The people who first told this story discovered what my late father discovered in the Jim Crow South. They discovered that we can experience new beginnings when our lives are shaped by a let-be God in a make-be world. That is the central claim of this chapter. It's about the capacity to imagine and experience that new beginnings are possible when our lives are being shaped by the let-be God. Our hope beyond the dead-end structures of this make-be world are determined by our commitment to worship and serve the let-be God. No matter how hopeless, troubling, and difficult life may be, everything changes when we shape our lives from the life-giving words of the let-be God.

The liturgical rhythm of this story is a God who responds to chaos by creating a new world with the words, *"Let there be."* In the midst of formlessness, emptiness, and darkness enters a God who transforms everything and creates something wonderfully new by saying, *"Let there be."* The most dominant character in the story is God, and the most creative words in the story are

God's words, "Let there be." God is the primary subject, and everything God does is a response to what God says, and creation and creatures are created when God says, *"Let there be."* Basic English teaches us that a sentence is in order when there is a subject, a verb, and an object. God is the subject. Creation is the object, or noun, but what connects subject and object is the verb, *"Let there be."*

In our recent First Things First Conference, Bishop Teal challenged us to consider that order is God's strategy for increase. Life's blessings inevitably flow toward people whose lives are in order. Genesis is a prophetic call to order. When life is out of order, you do well to return to the beginning. When life is being defined by the chaos of a make-be world, we are called to consider God's call to order, and we connect with God's order through new beginnings.

Consider the text. The first day was what I want to call first day theology. God said, *"Let there be light; and there was light."* To the darkness identified in verse 2, God created light, and God separated the light from the darkness. First day theology is God talk that separates light from darkness. Seeing new beginnings comes before living new beginnings. The second day is replete with second day theology. *"God said, 'Let there be a firmament.'"* In response to the emptiness cited in verse 2, God provided a firmament, and God called the firmament heaven. Second day theology is God talk that calls for faith in the midst of the uncontrollable. We must have faith, even in the midst of the uncontrollable.

The focus of this text is third day theology. It's a response to the third dynamic of chaos, which is formlessness, or as the text says, *"without form."* Light for the darkness. We have a firmament for the emptiness, and then form for formlessness.

God orders a distinction between the water and dry land, and purposefulness for the earth. God distinguished the waters and God called the dry land earth, and God called forth purposefulness from the earth. Third day theology is God talk that distinguishes and calls forth purposefulness.

The third day is the only day where God says, *"Let there be . . ."* twice. The first time God says let there be is to gather the waters together and let the dry land appear. Just as God separates light from darkness and separates the waters above from the waters below, God separates the waters from dry land. The people who wrote this text understood that people who need new beginnings also need separations. They knew that their world would never be formed in the order God intended as long as they stayed enmeshed in the make-be world dominated by their oppressor.

Likewise, we will never experience the world as God intends as long as we are connected to this make-be world. The make-be world is our attempt to make the world into something God never intended. The make-be world consists of human constructs to control, dominate, and exploit. The make-be world is our crazy beliefs that we can make people be what we want them to be; get them to do what we want them to do, and even make them believe what we want to them to believe. That's the problem with church life. Too much of church life is make-be, and sometimes make believe. We want to make people be Christian, make people be Baptist, Methodist, Disciple of Christ, Episcopalian, Presbyterian, and in the Islamic tradition, make them Arabic and then Muslim. We want to make people be holy, or make them be churchy.

The problem with some of our evangelism is that is make-be. We want to make people be what we want them to be, rather than for them to be who God intends for them to be. I recently read Dr. Martin Luther King's letter from a Birmingham jail. Dr. King noted that any law that deprives a person from experiencing the fullness of his or her life is unjust.

As a boy, whenever I felt the need to defy someone, I would say, "You can't make me." I would only use this strategy when it was someone I believed had no right telling me anything, or it was someone I thought I could hold my own against. (Obviously, that was never my father or mother.) However, what we are hearing from the millennials, or the younger generation, is a defiant, "You can't make me!" Black Lives Matter is defiance that's telling white America that you can't make black people accept state-sanctioned killing of black people.! Along with many well-meaning allies, African Americans are defiantly saying, "You can't make me accept my life being of less value than your life. You can't make me be ok with injustice, inequality, and brutality."

A day after the most recent United States presidential inauguration, women in fifty states and countries around the world gathered in one voice and said, "You can't make us accept Donald Trump as our president. You can't make us normalize someone who clearly isn't normal. You can't make us accept the dark world in his dark mind. You can't make us be mean, unloving, and selfish. You can't make us turn on one another, distrust one another, just because we are different. You can't make women accept men deciding what's best for women's bodies. You can't make us accept the rich getting richer and the poor getting poorer. You can't make us accept that eight people own as much wealth as half the world. We don't care how much America First rhetoric is espoused, you can't make us believe that this is what America is all about." The truth is, people of faith and good intent must insist that we have to separate ourselves from systems and powers of a make-be world. We have to separate ourselves from any and everything that's trying to make us be what we are not.

When the separation was made, the let-be God spoke again. God said, "Let the earth bring forth grass, the herb that yield seeds, and the fruit tree that yields fruity according to its kind, whose seed is in itself, on the earth and it was so."[41] Once things were in order, it was seed time. Seed time symbolizes the fulfillment of purpose. Every thing on the earth has a purpose to fulfill. Once things were in order, God called for purposefulness

---

41 Genesis 1:11

on the earth. Everything that has a seed, let it be what it's supposed to be. Let it bring forth what's in it, and every fruit bring forth the fruit that's within it. In other words, let each thing of the earth be what it was intended to be and quit trying to make it something it is not.

People who need new beginnings don't try to make the earth be something it is not, but allow the earth to be what it is. The earth is good, and has been created by a good God. The earth is not a tool to be exploited by the rich and powerful. The earth is not something we trash and pollute. Babylon, the gate of the gods, made gods of the earth. They made the people of God bow to the gods of the earth. Like America, they made people bow to stuff that came from the earth. They made earth things more popular than God, and earth stuff more attractive than worship.

Dr. J. Alfred Smith Sr. shared with me that black America is in exile. Exile is basically not being where you are supposed to be. The truth is, we are not where we are supposed to be. We are not being who we are supposed to be. We are not doing what we are supposed to do. Like the people in our text, we are living in a make-be world. Paul put it like this, "Do not be conformed to this world, but be transformed by the renewing of your mind."[42] Jesus said, "You are in the world, but not of the world."[43]

---

42 Romans 12:2a
43 John 17:16

While being overwhelmed by the gods of the make-be world, Isaiah and the other prophets sought to encourage God's people. In the midst of formlessness, Isaiah declared:

> Why do you say, O Jacob,
> And speak, O Israel:
> "My way is hidden from the LORD,
> And my just claim is passed over by my God"?
> Have you not known?
> Have you not heard?
> The everlasting God, the LORD,
> The Creator of the ends of the earth,
> Neither faints nor is weary.
> His understanding is unsearchable.
> He gives power to the weak,
> And to those who have no might He increases strength.
> Even the youths shall faint and be weary,
> And the young men shall utterly fall,
> But those who wait on the LORD
> Shall renew their strength;
> They shall mount up with wings like eagles,
> They shall run and not be weary,
> They shall walk and not faint.[44]

I encourage you, my brother. I encourage you, my sister. Let God be God and the light will shine forth in the darkness. Let God be God and God will provide us a firmament in the midst of the uncontrollable. Let God be God and no artificial

---

[44] Isaiah 40:27-31

construct can make you be what you were not created to be. Let God be God and you will have no need to try to make your brother, or make your sister, do anything against his or her will. Let God be God and the universe aligns up with you. Let God be God and God will take care of you.

<u>DISCUSSION MATTERS</u>

1. How did you react to the belief that the only thing black people represented in this nation were to "work for white people"? Do you believe this? If not, why not?
2. Are these areas in your faith experience where you saw a need for "theological expansion"?
3. Do you think it important to expand our talk about God in ways that impact how we live in the world?
4. The fact of formlessness calls for a creative impetus from who I call the "Let-be God", how liberating is that concept when living in a "make-be world"?
5. Are there instances, or experiences in your life, or your community, where you, or community, were forced to be someone you were not? Discuss.
6. Can you cite any social, or civil resistance, was a response to the "make-be" tendencies of our country?
7. Are there any make-be realties in your life, church, or world that welcomes the liberating impetus of a "Let-be God'?

CHAPTER 7

THE FOURTH DAY:
LIGHTS IN THE FIRMAMENT

TEXT: *"Then God said, 'Let there be lights in the firmament of the heavens to divide the day from the night; and let them be for signs and seasons, and for days and years; and let them be for lights in the firmament of the heavens to give light on the earth'; and it was so. Then God made two great lights: the greater light to rule the day, and the lesser light to rule the night. He made the stars also. God set them in the firmament of the heavens to give light on the earth, and to rule over the day and over the night, and to divide the light from the darkness. And God saw that it was good. So the evening and the morning were the fourth day" (Gen. 1:14–19).*

A Pre-Word: The evening of this day is the creature being forced to consider aspects of creation as being theologically equivalent to the Creator. While the sun and the moon are impressive aspects of creation, they were never intended to supplant God the Creator. When products of creation are elevated to the inimitable space of the Creator, the creature's potential for oppressive constructs are exacerbated. Sun and moon worship were theological impositions that further promoted the imperialistic practices of the Babylonian empire. As a consequence, the exiled masses were subjected to a colonized mindset that was theologically justified.

The morning, however, is the rejection of creation-based theology to the radical acceptance of a theology grounded in a loving Creator of "which everything that is made was made by Him." While much about the human experience may suggest aspects of domineering uncontrollability, the lights in the firmament represent creative expressions of a loving God who sides with the oppressed. How do we sort through theological confusion and discern the reality of a God who indisputably sides with the oppressed?

In 1972, a young artist performing under the name of Stevie Wonder had a number one hit entitled "Superstition." In a year when so many songs and artists captured the attention of America, "Superstition" held number one. Songs and artists like Roberta Flack's tantalizing, "The First Time Ever I Saw Your Face," Michael Jackson's "Rockin' Robin," Aretha Franklin's "Daydreaming," Bill Withers' "Lean On Me," AL Green's, "Still in Love With You," and "Look What You Done for Me." The Main Ingredient was singing "Everybody Plays a Fool." The O'Jays were on it with "Back Stabber," and Chuck Berry was merrily singing, "My Ding-A-Ling." Yet Stevie Wonder captured the attention of the world singing:

Very superstitious, writing on the wall

Very superstitious, ladders 'bout to fall

Thirteen month old baby, broke the lookin' glass

Seven years of bad luck, the good things in your past

> When you believe in things that you don't understand
> Then you suffer
> Superstition ain't the way.

In a world with so many superstitions, the people of God need to heed Stevie's words, "Superstition ain't the way." Stevie Wonder believed it critical that if we are going to live authentic lives of faith, superstition is not the way. If we are going to truly be the people of God, superstition is not the way. If we are going to have a credible witness for a skeptical generation, superstition is not the way. If God is going to be real in our lives, we don't need to be making stuff up, because superstition is not the way.

The people who wrote the words of our text were caught in a world, much like ours, where superstitious understandings of life, the world, and God were being imposed upon them. They were being indoctrinated into a worldview that justified their oppression, and religious constructs gave the oppressors religious legitimacy. It was in this context that they decided superstition was not the way. As a result, they rejected the worldview of their oppressor that delegitimized them and decided to shape their lives on the life-changing belief that the world was definitively created by God. While superstitions had folks worshipping the sun and the moon, they determined that God created the sun and the moon. They decided that they needed a new beginning beyond superstitions and embraced the belief that God placed the lights in the firmament.

That's what the fourth day is all about. Therefore, I want to propose to sophisticated, intelligent, technocratic people of the twenty-first century that our new beginnings are predicated upon the faithful embrace of the lights in the firmament. I know you are smart. I know you are technologically savvy and culturally sophisticated, but I invite you to sit for a minute in the creation drama of new beginnings.

Again, the people who wrote this text understood, as we need to understand, that to be freed of superstitions requires a God-shift. They shifted from the gods of their oppressors, which included worshipping the sun and the moon, and declared,

> New-beginning possibilities demand that we shape a story with God as the Creator, and not Pharaoh, Nebuchadnezzar, Belshazzar, Caesar—and especially not Donald J. Trump.

"In the beginning God created the heavens and the earth." Without the creative impetus and power of God, they noted that the earth was without form, and void, and darkness was upon the face of the deep.

I'm rallied by this ancient story, known as the Creation Story, which is really the Creator story, or God-talk for creation. I'm rallied because it provides new-beginning possibilities for people who need them. New-beginning possibilities demand that we shape a story with God as the Creator, and not Pharaoh, Nebuchadnezzar, Belshazzar, Caesar—and especially not Donald J. Trump.

During the winter and early spring of each year, we are alerted of the flu season. We are alerted and to protect the masses from the flu, flu shots are offered. It's not a matter of whether or not the flu is coming. The flu will be present. The flu breaks out everywhere, and the question is, are you going to be immune?

The Creation Story provides oppressed people with spiritual immunization from what is obvious in our world, which is the demonic influence of powers in high places. On the first day, God dealt with the darkness by creating light. On the second day, God dealt with the emptiness, the void, by creating a firmament. God created a firmament in the midst of the waters. On the third day, God dealt with the lack of form by gathering up the waters and letting the dry land appear. And God called forth the grass, herbs, and the fruit. In dramatic order, God separated disorder and set order.

The fourth day is about God positioning life sources, and the primary source for life is light. For there to be life, there must first be light. So God said, "Let there be lights in the firmament."[45] In the firmament, God placed the lights. In the dome, God created lights. In the place God called heaven, God created light. Life-giving forces were placed in the firmament and the lights have specific functions, to divide the night from the day, set the timing for the seasons, and provide the calendaring process for days and years. Life functions in seasons, and our seasons are determined by light.

---

45 Genesis 1:14

At the writing of this chapter, we were in winter, and during the winter, nights are longer than the day. You can spring your clock forward and fall back all you want, the nights will still be longer than the days, because of the lights in the firmament. Some of us have had some winter seasons in our lives, where the nights were painfully longer than the days. Some of us might even be in a winter season right now. I consider this a winter season for America. Gill Scott-Heron once prophetically sang, "It's winter in America."[46] Yet, the good news of this text is that even in night, God has placed a light in the firmament. People who need new beginnings must embrace the liberating power of lights in the firmament. It doesn't matter how dark, or how long the darkness; God has placed lights in the firmament. It doesn't matter how difficult life may seem, God has placed lights in the firmament.

We need to get this because the people who wrote this text had much longer than four or eight years of darkness. They had years of the darkness. They had so many years that Isaiah was asked, "Watchman, what of the night?"[47] They had so many years of the darkness that Jeremiah told them to build homes in the darkness. Marry your sons and daughters in the darkness. Plant crops, set up camp, because we are going to be in this darkness for a long time. Bless the city where you are because it's blessing will be your blessing.[48] We are going to be in this darkness so long that some people are going to get used to the

---

46 Winter In America, Gil Scott-Heron, 1974
47 Isaiah 21:11
48 Jeremiah 29:5-7

darkness. Some of the Lord's people are going to be so accustomed to the darkness that they will normalize the darkness. Yet, the people of faith will hold on because they understood that even in the darkness God has lights in the firmament. God has so arranged the world that there is a light, a life source, even in the darkness.

The other day, Eugene Cernan died. Eugene Cernan was an astronaut, and was the last man to walk on the moon. Guess what year he last walked? In 1972, the same year that Stevie Wonder's "Superstition" hit number one on the charts, Eugene Cernan walked on the moon. We have not had another person on the moon since 1972; not because of Stevie's song, but primarily because it was determined that the moon could never sustain life. The only life-giving opportunity for the moon was the light it reflected in the night. "God made two great lights: the greater light to rule the say, and the lesser light to rule the night."[49] While the moon provides light in the night, it is not a source of light. The sun is the source of light. The moon reflects the light provided by the sun.

Now the people who wrote this text did not have a Eugene Cernan. They did not even have a telescope, let alone an astronaut and a spaceship. Yet, they understood something that John later articulates. "In the beginning was the Word and the Word was with God, and the Word was God. And He was in the beginning with God. All things were made through Him, and without Him nothing was made that was made. In Him

---
49 Genesis 1:16

was life, and the life was the light of men. And shines in darkness, and the darkness did not comprehend it. There was a man sent from God, whose name was John. This man came for a witness, to bear witness of the light, that all through him might believe. He was not the light, but was sent to bear witness of that Light."[50]

I'm done, but I am not finished. We are living in a dark season. We are living in a time when we are being asked to confuse light with darkness, wrong with right. I don't know about you, but I'm going to do like John and Stevie. I am not going to be superstitious. Superstitious is not the way. I'm clear about some things, and one thing I know is that I'm not the Light. I'm not the source of the light. The Son is the Light. The Son is the Light source for you and me. Jesus is the Light, and God has placed him in the firmament. Jesus came in the midst of the uncontrollable. The Bible says, "And the Word became flesh and dwelt among us, and we beheld his glory, the glory of the only begotten of the Father."[51]

Jesus came in the midst of the meanness, in the midst of the racism, in the midst of the xenophobia, the greed, and the cruelty. Jesus came and declared, "I am the light of the world."[52] He is the Source of the light, but we are called to be the reflection of his Light. Like the moon, we are not the source. Like John, we are not the Light, but we reflect the Light. We let the world

---

50 John 1:1-8
51 John 1:14
52 John 8:12

see the Light in us. In the firmament, let Jesus shine through us. Let his love shine through us. Let his joy shine through us. Let his power shine through us.

Oh, I can better hear my enslaved ancestors. I hear better those whipped-back brothers and those bent-back sisters who, in the midst of the darkness of slavery; in the midst of Jim Crow; in the midst of midnight rapes and daytime lynchings, they sang:

This little light of mine, I'm going to let it shine.

Everywhere I go, I'm going to let it shine.

I can't make it shine, but I'm going to let it shine.

Let is shine, let it shine, let it shine.

In the firmament, let it shine.

In my neighborhood, I'm going to let it shine."

DISCUSSION MATTERS

1. Stevie Wonder believed it critical that if we are going to live authentic lives of faith, superstition is not the way. What are your thoughts?

2. Are there any prevailing superstitions functioning in your life? Church? family? What are they?

3. How does a God-shift address life-defeating superstitions?

4. Respond to the assertion that "the fourth day is about God positioning life sources, and the primary source for life is light."

5. How has "darkness" been normalized in our world?

6. What are some of the darksome areas in our world that could benefit from "lights in the firmament"?

7. Are you motivated to be a reflection of Him who claimed to be "the Light of the World"? How so?

CHAPTER 8

THE FIFTH DAY:
THE OVER-AND-UNDER GOD

TEXT: *"Then God said, 'Let the waters abound with an abundance of living creatures, and let birds fly above the earth across the face of the firmament of the heavens.' So God created great sea creatures and every living thing that moves, with which the waters abounded, according to their kind, and every winged bird according to its kind. And God saw that it was good. And God blessed them, saying, 'Be fruitful and multiply, and fill the waters in the seas, and let birds multiply on the earth.' So the evening and the morning were the fifth day"* (Gen. 1:20–23).

A Pre-Word: Nothing has provoked as much creature-envy than the capacity of birds to fly sky high and fish to swim the ocean deep, all doing so without artificial aids. The evening of this day highlights how creature-envy promotes a god-complex that shows up in humanity's inhumanity to other human beings, as well as the exploitation of land, air, and sea. The god-complex that deludes oppressors finds them creating human images and likenesses that anthropomorphize air and sea-born creatures to the detriment of all creation. Imposing a belief system that justifies the exploitation of the earth eventually destroys the earth, as well as its inhabitants.

The morning comes when the creatures acknowledge that the "earth is the Lord's and fullness thereof, and all who dwell therein."[53] Creator-based faith provides the creatures a stewardship perspective that honors creation as a gift and not as an object to be abused and exploited. Honoring the air and sea subsequently honors all of life, inclusive of one's fellow human beings. How do we shape a faith perspective that honors creation as a gift?

Whatever else the opening pages of the Bible ought to teach us is that creativity happens in tension. God does God's best work within tensions. Even within the drama of creation we are invited to consider creative tensions. There is first God and then there is chaos. There is formlessness, emptiness, and darkness. Hovering over the chaos is the Spirit of God, positioning God's self for creative possibilities. For the darkness, God creates light. For the emptiness, or the void, God creates a firmament. For the formlessness, God gathered up the waters and let dry land appear.

The fifth day invites us into the tension of over and under. The God who creates calls us to creative living when we embrace the creative tensions of over and under. It does not matter your lot in life, how well you are doing or how bad life might be, we are all dealing with some over and under stuff. Therefore, I want to propose that new beginnings are possible when we acknowledge and embrace a faith in the tension of the over and under.

---

53 Psalm 24:1

This text teaches us that people of faith encounter God within the tension of over and under because God is an over-and-under God.

Creative living is the result of creating in the tension. We grow stronger in tension. We become wiser in tension. We get better in tension. We become courageous through challenge, and become more loving through heartache and pain. If we want to do anything with our darkness, my Tennessee pastor, Dr. Amos Jones Jr., told us, "Don't curse the darkness, but light a candle in the dark." For eight years we witnessed Barak Obama, the first African-American president of America, engage in creative living in the midst of tension. While racist obstructionists fought him on every hand, he never reduced himself to their level. Each time they went low, he went high. Obama served eight years scandal-free, while Trump has been scandalous throughout his nasty campaign and two years in office.

The Creator Story teaches us that if we want to do anything with our emptiness, let's hold to our faith in the midst of the firmament. If we want to do anything with our lack of form, let's gather up and separate what we can't control from what we can control. In Reinhold Neihbur's prayer, now used as the serenity prayer, he prayed:

> God, give us grace to accept with serenity
>
> the things that cannot be changed,
>
> Courage to change the things

> which should be changed,
>
> and the Wisdom to distinguish
>
> the one from the other.

If we want to see something come out of our chaos, let's allow our lives to be shaped by the Spirit. That's what the people did who wrote our text. Read Exodus 1, verse 12, "The more they afflicted them, the more they multiplied and grew." They allowed the Spirit of God to create for them new beginnings in the midst of their chaos. They embraced a faith in the over-and-under God.

In reality, the days of our lives are lived in tension. When we went to school, we learned how to count, but when we came to church, we learned how to pray. When we went to school, we learned how to think, but when we came to church, we learned how to believe. When we went to school, we were taught to solve problems, but when we came to church, we were exhorted to "walk by faith and not by sight."[54] When we went to school, we were supposed to learn how to negotiate living in the world of competing realities, but when we came to church, we were taught how to live a life of faith. When we went to school, we were told that math and science rule, but when we came to church, we learned that God rules, and super-rules.

The world teaches us that the only thing that truly matters is money, material, and might, but that's not spiritual living.

---

54 2 Corinthians 5:7

We are now being told to Make America Great Again, but Jesus taught that the greatest is the least. We are being told make America first, but Jesus taught the first shall be last and the last shall be first. We are being told to be tough, but Jesus told us to be wise as a serpent and gentle as a dove. Clearly, we are at our best when we live from the perspective of the spiritual. We are more of who we were created to be when in relationship with the One who created us to be. We are our best selves when we connect with the One who addresses our problems of darkness with his marvelous light. We are more complete when we relate with the One who addresses our emptiness by filling us with his Spirit. We are more of who we are meant to be when our problem of formlessness is addressed by the One who can mold us and shape us into useful vessels.

I teach that there is no loose change in the Bible. There is nothing within the biblical story that we can dispose of and dismiss as lacking in significance. Consider the issue of numbers in the Bible. I have long held that numbers have meaning. Numbers have such profound meaning within the Bible that there is a whole book entitled Numbers. I once outlined a perspective on the number three in the Creator story, commonly referred to as the Creation Story. However, this text focuses on the fifth day. Just as number 3 denotes wholeness or completeness, number 5 is the number for grace. We are created with five fingers, five toes, five senses, and if we live long enough, we should have five seasons of life: the infant season, the child season, the adolescent season, the adult season, and the senior season. Yet, all that we are and all that we have is because the grace of God shows up in the tension of the over and under.

Again, Bishop Teal taught us that order is God's strategy for increase. God sets things in order. God took three days to deal with three problems: the problem of darkness, the problem of emptiness, and the problem of formlessness. The first three days are days of preparation and the next three are days of population. In increments of threes, God prepares and then God populates. God prepares the world for life and then God populates the world with life. However, on the fifth day, the day of grace, we encounter something incredible. We encounter the liberating tension of living with the up and under God. The let-be God reveals God's self as the up and under God. God said, "Let the waters abound with an abundance of living creatures, and let the birds fly above the earth across the face of the firmament of the heavens." So God created great seas creatures and every living thing that moves, with which the water abounded, according to their kind, and every winged bird according to its kind. And God saw that it was good."[55]

In a world where people worshipped birds and fashioned sky gods, spiritual people defied the norm and declared that every thing flying in the air was created by God. The same people who worshipped the things that flew over the earth, violently imposed their will over other people on the earth. In a world

---

[55] Genesis 1:20-21

where people worshipped sea creatures and had sea gods, spiritual people defied the norm and declared that everything in the sea was created by God. The same people who worshipped the things under the water did all they could to put other people under them. Yet, the people who wrote this text declared that which existed above the earth and that which existed under the sea—it all was created by God! The birds are over and the great sea creatures are under, but God created them all.

Estelle Frankel notes that the ancient Hebrews believed that healing and creation go together.[56] The people who wrote our text understood that for healing to take place, it involves the process of re-creation. The healing of an oppressed people from the brutal experiences of Exodus and Exile demanded the construction of a new cosmogony, or the formulating of a Creation Story that featured a Creator God. In a world distorted by an array of oppressive idolatry, they carefully and meticulously designed a story of new beginnings for people who needed them.

When the oppressed people of God considered life, they knew, as we should know, that oppressed people are always being subjected to the tensions of over and under. In fact, oppression is maintained and sustained by systems and structures that are over and under. We are overcome, and then we are underrepresented. We are overworked and underpaid. We are overburdened and underappreciated. We are overcharged and underrated. We are overwhelmed and underprivileged. We are

---

56 Op. cite, Frankel, pp. 10-11

overstressed and underinsured. We are overloaded and underestimated. We are overruled and undercut. Our shortcomings are overblown and our strengths underexposed. We overborrow and underinvest. We overcompensate and are underdeveloped. We overeat and are undernourished. We overdose and are undertaken by the undertaker, who overcharges to put us under the ground. Something or someone is always over us, and we are always under something or under someone.

Yet the testimony of this text is that everything that is over us and everything that is under us, God can use it to bless us. It's in the text! God still prepares and God still populates. God sets in order that every created thing that is over and under, God uses for increase. "And God blessed them, saying, 'Be fruitful and multiply, and fill the waters in the seas, and let birds multiply on the earth.' And the evening and the morning was the fifth day."

Here is the morning hope to the evening reality: whatever has been over us and whatever has been under us, God wants to use it to bless us. The over-and-under God called forth blessings from the things that were over and the things that were under. The over-and-under God produced fruit from the over and the under; the sun over, the seed in the soil is under. Wherever the Spirit of the Lord is, a blessing is possible. That's what the psalmists declared when they sang, "Where can I go from Your Spirit? Or, where can I flee from Your presence? If I ascend into heaven, You are there; if I make my bed in hell, behold, You are there. If I take the wings of the morning, and dwell in the uttermost parts of the sea, even there Your hand shall lead me, and Your right hand shall hold me. If I say, ,Surely the darkness shall fall on me, even the night shall be light about me; indeed, the darkness shall not hide me from You, but the night shines as the darkness; the darkness and the light are both alike to You.'"[57]

Paul would later write, "Yet in all these things we are more than conquerors through Him who loved us. For I am persuaded that neither death nor life, nor angels, nor principalities nor powers, nor things present nor things to come, nor height nor depth, nor any other created things, shall be able to separate us from the love of God which is in Christ Jesus our Lord."[58]

We don't sing it much anymore, but we used to sing:

> Well, He's so high (so high you can't get over Him)
>
> So wide (so wide you can't get around Him)
>
> So low (so low you can't get under him)
>
> Great God Almighty (you must come in at the door)

The good news, or the morning hope for all who are being subjected to overwhelming and undervaluing realities, is a faith perspective that God is higher than high and lower than low. There is no oppressive construct or demonic reality that supplants or replaces the over-and-under God. In the faith perspective of the over-and-under God, whatever holds us down will

---

[57] Psalm 139:7-12
[58] Romans 8:37-39

be lifted and whatever falsely lifts us up shall be brought down. Praise God, because the high shall be brought low and the low shall be set high, "and all flesh shall see it together." "And the evening and the morning was the fifth day."

DISCUSSION MATTERS

1. What are your thoughts on the assertion that "God does God's best work within tensions"? Have there been tensions in your life where something creative was produced? Discuss.

2. The author believes that "all that we are and all that we have is because the grace of God shows up in the tension of the over and under." What are your thoughts?

3. Do you agree with the assertion that "oppression is maintained and sustained by systems and structures that are over and under"? How expressed?

4. Can you see, as does Estelle Frankel where "creation and healing" go together? Discuss.

5. Are there moments in your life, church, or community where that which was over us and under us was used by God to bless us?

CHAPTER 9

THE SIXTH DAY:
JUST LIKE GOD

TEXT: *"Then God said, 'Let the earth bring forth the living creature according to its kind: cattle and creeping thing and beast of the earth, each according to its kind'; and it was so. And God made the beast of the earth according to its kind, cattle according to its kind, and everything that creeps on the earth according to its kind. And God saw that it was good. Then God said, 'Let Us make man in Our image, according to Our likeness; let them have dominion over the fish of the sea, over the birds of the air, and over the cattle, over all the earth and over every creeping thing that creeps on the earth.' So God created man in His own image; in the image of God He created him; male and female He created them. Then God blessed them, and God said to them, 'Be fruitful and multiply; fill the earth and subdue it; have dominion over the fish of the sea, over the birds of the air, and over every living thing that moves on the earth.'*

"And God said, 'See, I have given you every herb that yields seed which is on the face of all the earth, and every tree whose fruit yields seed; to you it shall be for food. Also, to every beast of the earth, to every bird of the air, and to everything that creeps on the earth, in which there is life, I have given every green herb for food'; and it was so. Then God saw everything that He had made, and indeed it was very good. So the evening and the morning were the sixth day" (Gen. 1:24–31).

A Pre-Word: The evening of the sixth day represents the dominant issue that promotes inhumanity, cruelty, and inequity. Our proclivity to elevate and idolatrize bestialized humanity continues to sustain racism, sexism, injustice, violence, and every evil expression of social and global oppression. The inability to acknowledge and embrace the humanity of another, no matter how different he or she might be, darkens our capacity to be just and humane. Every act of injustice, cruelty, and oppression can be traced to the evening of idolatrous constructs of human bestiality, ethnocentrism, and racial arrogance. When life is shaped by idolatrous constructs we forfeit our opportunity to be just like God.

While we are not God, we have been endowed with God-like potential to be more than what we are. Hence, the morning of the sixth day is for us to consider one another as creatures made in the image and likeness of God. God invests God in the human creature! Unlike the other land-bound creatures, we can rise above our bestial instincts and become life-giving entities just like God. What might the challenges be that hinder us from being just like God?

The story is told that Mary Mcleod Bethune, a child of former slaves, was stumping around the country to raise money for the fledgling school she founded with five students, the Daytona Normal and Industrial Institute for Girls, which would later go coed and become Bethune-Cookman College. She knocked on the door of a prominent Methodist preacher and a little girl answered the door. Mary Mcleod Bethune asked the young girl a question that would set the trajectory of the young girl's life. Madame Bethune asked her, "Who you're going to be?" Not what you are going to be? Or, what you are going to do? But, who are you going to be?

The young girl was Leontyne Kelly, who would become the first African-American woman to become a bishop within the predominantly white United Methodist Church. I had the pleasure of meeting Leontyne Kelly while matriculating at Vanderbilt Divinity School. Leontyne Kelly would testify that she spent her life answering that question, and determined who she was going to be would not be determined by what the society said she could be, but who God called her to be.

The question raised by Mary Mcleod Bethune seemed to have been one that drove the people who crafted the genius of the Creation narratives. While lingering in the dehumanizing pits of Babylonian exile, the oppressed people of God knew that whoever they were going to be depended upon who God was going to be in their lives. They knew, as we should know, that a people never become who they are going to be until there's some clarity about who God is going to be.

In a world of darkness, emptiness, and formlessness, they sought to re-story who God was going to be in defiance to who their oppressors had made God to be. God was not the moon, the sun, or the stars. God created the moon, the sun, and the stars. God was not the trees, plants, the fish in the sea, nor anything that crawled upon the face of the earth. God created the trees, the plants, the fish in the sea, and everything that crawled upon the face of the earth. I remember vividly how the late Reverend John Malone would pray with tear-stained eyes:

"O God, the cattle on a thousand hills are Thine. The fish that swim the mighty deep are Thine. The birds that plume through the air are Thine. The silver and the gold are Thine. And we your land-bound creatures are Thine, also."[59]

In a spirit of defiance to the false claims of a dehumanizing society, he would continue praying, "We, who walk the earth are Thine, also." (Oh, I how I've bemoaned not recording that incredible prayer!)

While walking through the San Francisco International Airport, I noted a display entitled, Caticons: The Cat In Art. My curiosity to understand why cats warranted such noted public mention led me to read the advertising plaque. Having serious resistance to cat ownership, I learned that cats were once worshipped by ancient Egyptians and other civilizations. Even the Prophet Muhammad, peace be upon him, was known to have a great affinity for cats. More significant is the fact that archeological findings of animal masks and artifacts reveal that animal worship was quite common.

John Calvin aptly defined the human mind as "a perpetual factory of idols."[60] Competitive sports may well represent an idolatrous extension of this animalistic impulse to worship "our" teams bearing names such as the Eagles, Bears, Lions,

---

59 Prayer offered at the New Saint James Baptist Church, Richmond, CA, 1979
60 Calvin, John, Institutes of the Christian Religion Vol. 2

Cubs, Hawks, Bulls, etc., where we regale in dominating, demolishing, and destroying rivals. (Interestingly, most professional teams are owned by billionaires who thrive in the dog-eat-dog of Western capitalism.)

> Theologically, we become what we worship, and bestiality functions to dehumanize, demean, and objectify human beings.

Theologically, we become what we worship, and bestiality functions to dehumanize, demean, and objectify human beings. The evening of dehumanizing constructs and systems happens when bestiality shapes and informs the socio-political landscape. The morning comes when our common humanity emerges and we are able to see that each one of us as being just like God.

Therefore, when we enter into the sixth day, the final day of God's creative activity, the oppressed people of God sought to make it plain that God did something extra when God created human beings. Again, human beings were not the only thing created on the sixth day. Human beings were not even the first thing created on the sixth day. God created every living creature: cattle, and creeping (not creepy) things, and beasts of the earth. Human beings were created on creature-creating day. Human beings are creatures fashioned by the Creator, but God dignified human beings by creating them, male and female, in God's likeness and image. In other words, God enhanced us with God-ness and God made us just like God.

The idea driving our conversation on the sixth day is that people who need new beginnings must possess a self-understanding that is just like God. The potential for new beginnings is bound to our commitment to possess a self-understanding that is just like God. We position ourselves to becoming all that God created us to be when we embrace the stubborn belief that the God who creates the earth, the sun, the moon, the sky, the stars in the firmament, the seed for grass, flowers, fish in the sea, cattle on the hills, and every other creature, dignified us with an essence that is just like God. "Then God said, 'Let us make man in Our image, according to Our likeness.'"[61]

The theologians would later term it "imago dei," the God image. The psalmist would later lift to liturgical melody: "For you formed my inward parts; You covered me in my mother's womb. I will praise You, for I am fearfully and wonderfully made; marvelous are Your works, and that my soul knows very well. How precious also are Your thoughts to me, O God! How great is the sum of them."[62] The artist would later stroke genius with the eyes of a child and declare, "I know I'm somebody, because God doesn't make any junk."

Oh, how transformative this message could be to a people whose lives have been defined by an oppressive self-understanding! What a difference this message could make in the lives of young men and women of color who seem to take pride in being so unlike God! When you are just like God, you resist and re-

---
61 Genesis 1:26
62 Psalm 139:13-14, 17

fute bestial behavior, even within one's self. When you believe you are just like God, you don't find it becoming, cool, or acceptable to be called someone's dog. When you believe that you are just like God, you don't do stupid things that allow people to put you in a cage like an animal. When you internalize that you are just like God, you never settle for being a b-i-t-c-h. When you know that you are like God, you give some thought to how you show up in the world, and you do your best to show up just like God.

One of the things that drove our people to leave en masse from the Jim Crow South was they knew they were not niggers, coons, boys, and heifers. While the Constitution of the United States of America declared that blacks were only three-fifths human, the old slave preacher would dignify the enslaved with the words, "I have a new name over in glory, and it's mine, mine, all mine."

In 2017, the year was promoted as the Crisis in Education for African Americans. It was noted that "Throughout the last quarter of the twentieth century and continuing today, the crisis in black education has grown significantly in urban neighborhoods where public schools lack resources, endure overcrowding, exhibit a racial achievement gap, and confront policies that fail to deliver substantive opportunities. The touted benefits of education remain elusive to many blacks of all ages. Tragically, some poorly performing schools serve as pipelines to prison for youths."[63]

---

63 UC Davis Health, Cultural News, Volume 15, Issue 2, Feb. 2017

The Church may well have to assume responsibility for educating black children, because there's nothing to suggest that things in public education will get better anytime soon. This will not be a new experience. Most of our migrant parents and grandparents were educated in a church building that served as the schoolhouse during the week. The only thing different is that we will have the freedom to shape the curriculum and select the teachers. We need a new beginning where our children will know that they are just like God.

What does this text teach us about what it means to an oppressed people to embrace a self-understanding of being just like God? Just as the oppressed people of God used this text to re-image themselves into a new beginning, we, too, can begin where they began. They began by noting that everything God made was good. Each day in creation is noted that God saw that it was good. Light is good. The dry land and the sea is good. The grass, the fruit on the tree, the sun, and the moon was good. The birds and the fish were good. The cattle and the beasts were good. In other words, everything that God created is "all good!"

Notice, they are not God. They are good. The word used for good actually means it is usable, or that it matters. We are like God when we concur that the things of this world, including in the sky, are not God, but it all matters. There ought to be a curiosity about the world that inspires research among our people. We should not be content with other people telling us what the world is. We need to find out for ourselves what the world is and how one thing relates to another. It ought to matter so much that we don't use the things of the earth to do something they never were intended to do. I'm sorry you all, I am a conservationist. I believe that this world is a good world and it can be good for a long time, if we treat it like it matters. We don't need to use it up, hog it up, burn it up, mess it up, blow it up, gas it up, or tear it up and destroy the world in our generation. When we are like God, we treat the world like it's God's.

I don't care how you read the Bible, particularly the Creation Story; there is nothing there that suggests God gave us the world to do whatever we want to do with it. The psalmist dittos the God-ness of the world when singing, "The earth is the Lord's and the fullness thereof, and they that dwell therein."[64] We are just like God when the care of the world matters to us just as it matters to God.

We are just like God when we view others as being just like God. While living in Brooklyn, we used a greeting at the Saint Paul Community Baptist Church. The greeting was, "Namaste." Namaste is Hindu Sanskrit for the "the divinity in me greets the divinity in you." Consider verse 27 of Genesis. I believe it is one of the most ignored texts in the Bible. Men, in particular, like to skip over verse 27 in chapter 1 and focus on verse 22 in chapter 2, and then we misread it. (We like the rib story, rather than the image and likeness story.) Verse 27 reads: "So God created man in his image; in the image of God He created him; male and

---

64 Psalm 24:1

female He created them." The word used for *man* is "adam", or humankind. Adam, or humankind, was created in relationship with opposites; "male and female He created them." In God's image, both created by God. In other words, men and women are just like God.

We are just like God when relationships among sexes matter. To really get this, we need to hear this from the voices of oppressed people. People who are oppressed usually find someone they can oppress. Oppressed black men, including religious black men, oppress women. However, this text destroys any of our notions to make women less than men, and for that matter, to make any other person less than someone else. Black people and white people are just like God. Brown people and yellow people are just like God. It would take a Jesus to come along to help us to hear this when his missionary itinerary dictated that he must need go through Samaria, and while there, engaged in a public conversation with a woman. The Samaritans had been historically viewed as racially less than Jews, and women had been considered genetically less than men. I heard an imaginative white women preacher colorfully note that in this text we find "a man somewhere where he should not have been, doing something he should not have been doing, talking to someone he should not have been talking to, about matters he should not have been talking to her about."[65]

We are just like God when we don't place ourselves over other people, and when we don't put people on a pedestal where

---

[65] Anna Carter Florence preaching during the Festival of Homiletics, 2017

they don't belong. White supremacy and black inferiority have no standing in the world when you are just like God. Male chauvinism and female subjectivism has no place in our families when we are just like God. Objectification of children and women are not viable options when we are just like God.

Since I'm this close, I might as well say it. How one people worship God is no better than how other people worship God when we understand that we are all just like God. Christian elitism is a corrosive construct created by the Church to justify its inhumane treatment of other people for the sake of colonialism. Christian elitism otherizes people, and when we otherize people, we are unlike God. For when we don't view other people as being just like God, we do things that are unlike God. We believe ourselves to be justified in banning others, making slaves out of others, exterminating others, bombing others, detaining others, incarcerating others, walling out others, kidnapping and destroying others.

Finally, when we are just like God, we want to do as God does, which is to be a blessing. It's in the text! "Then God blessed them, and God said to them, 'Be fruitful and multiply; fill the earth and subdue it; have dominion over the fish of the sea, over the birds of the air, and over every living thing, that moves on the earth.'"[66] Some of us, when we read this part of the text, thought it referred exclusively to having children. We've even distorted and objectified marriage to be for mating, breeding,

---

66 Genesis 1:28

having children. A marriage constructed just for children is an assault upon the humanity of the man and the woman, to say nothing about how harmful it is to children! The text actually refers to using the creative energy that God has invested in us to make the world better, more beautiful, and more useful.

One of the great teachings of Jesus was that Jesus provided us an image that was just like God. It took Jesus to get us to see that we are just like God. Jesus told his disciples, "If you have seen me, you have seen the Father."[67] There's a whole book in the New Testament dedicated to this Christological idea. In Paul's letter to the Colossians, he writes:

> He has delivered us from the power of darkness and conveyed us into the kingdom of the Son of His love, in whom we have redemption through His blood, the forgiveness of sins. He is the image of the invisible God, the firstborn over all creation. For by Him all things were created that are in heaven and that are on earth, visible and invisible, whether thrones or dominions or principalities or powers. All things were created through Him and for Him. And He is before all things, and in Him all things consist. And He is the head of the body, the Church, who is the beginning, the firstborn from the dead, that in all things He may have the preeminence.[68]

---

67 John 14:9
68 Colossians 1:13-18

I don't know how the enslavers of black people and the killers of red people missed this verse. There is nothing in the verse that suggests having dominion over other people. There's nothing in this text about killing people, colonizing people, or stealing other people's land. I believe that if we embrace the self-image of being just like God, we can use our respective gifts and talents to make the world better for all people.

It took a Stevie Wonder to sing into our hearts that it took people of all races, creeds, and colors to make this world what it is. Stevie sang:

> First man to die
> For the flag we now hold high [*Crispus Attucks*]
> Was a black man
>
> The ground were we stand
> With the flag held in our hand
> Was first the red man's
>
> Guide of a ship
> On the first Columbus trip [*Pedro Alonzo Nino*]
> Was a brown man
>
> The railroads for trains
> Came on tracking that was laid
> By the yellow man
>
> We pledge allegiance
> All our lives
> To the magic colors

Red, blue and white
But we all must be given
The liberty that we defend
For with justice not for all men
History will repeat again
It's time we learned
This World Was Made For All Men

Heart surgery
Was first done successfully
By a black man [*Dr Daniel Hale Williams*]

Friendly man who died
But helped the pilgrims to survive [*Squanto*]
Was a red man

Farm workers rights
Were lifted to new heights [*Caesar Chavez*]
By a brown man

Incandescent light
Was invented to give sight [*Thomas Edison*]
By the white man

Now I know the birthday of a nation
Is a time when a country celebrates
But as your hand touches your heart
Remember we all played a part in America
To help that banner wave

First clock to be made
In America was created
By a black man [*Benjamin Banneker*]

Scout who used no chart
Helped lead Lewis and Clark
Was a red man [*Sacagawea*]

Use of martial arts
In our country got its start
By a yellow man

And the leader with a pen
Signed his name to free all men
Was a white man [*Abraham Lincoln*]

We pledge allegiance
All our lives
To the magic colors
Red, blue and white
But we all must be given
The liberty that we defend
For with justice not for all men
History will repeat again
It's time we learned
This World Was Made For All Men[69]

---

69 Stevie Wonder, Black Man 1976

DISCUSSION MATTERS

1. If we are not being and behaving "just like God," who are being like?

2. The author asserts that, "Every act of injustice, cruelty, and oppression can be traced to the evening of idolatrous constructs of human bestiality, ethnocentrism, and racial arrogance. Do you agree? If not, why not?

3. Can you embrace the assertion that "the idea driving our conversation on the sixth day is that people who need new beginnings must possess a self-understanding that is just like God"? Discuss.

4. In what ways has America demeaned people by distorting their humanity with oppressive self-understandings?

5. How has white supremacy and black inferiority distorted our humanity as being something other than just like God?

6. What are some ways we can created a new story for our humanity that aligns us as beings who are just like God?

CHAPTER 10

THE SEVENTH DAY:
A TIME FOR GOD

TEXT: *"Thus the heavens and earth, and all the hosts were finished. And on the seventh day God ended His work which He had done, and He rested on the seventh day from all His work which He had done. Then God blessed the seventh day and sanctified it, because in He rested from His work which God had created and made" (Gen. 2:1–3).*

A Pre-Word: Of note is the absence of the cadence "the evening and morning" on the seventh day. The Sabbath, as it is known, is initially designated as different.. Clearly, the Sabbath represented something different, and a break of order from the bustling socio-economic concerns of the previous days. There is a textual hush in the language of creation. In fact, the creation, or its creatures, are not even featured on the seventh day. The primary feature of the seventh day is God. The seventh day is dominated by one reality, the Creation God resting from creative busyness. Abraham Joshua Heschel noted that "Judaism is a religion of time aiming at the sancitification of time."[70] What's more needed of us than to prepare time in our lives dedicated to God?

---

70 Heschel, Abraham Joshua, *"The Sabbath*, (New York: Farrar, Straus and Geroux, 1952, 1979, 2005) p.8

I once visited a woman whose house was so neat and orderly that it made me nervous. While her company was pleasant, I could never relax and be myself because the meticulous tidiness of her house unnerved me. It wasn't her issue, or her fault. It was all me! Admittedly, I felt too internally tacky to sit in her overly neat space. The soil embedded within my psycho-spiritual construct would not allow me to be comfortable within her fastidious surroundings. I would later learn that she was a manic practitioner of feng shui.

For those interested, feng shui is a popular practice borrowed from the ancient Chinese. Feng shui has to do with the removal of clutter from one's life so that life-giving energy can flow more freely. Obviously, to maintain a culture to facilitate a billion people, the energy needs to flow. I purchased a book on feng shui that I really need to read, and certainly need to practice. I confess I need feng shui in my life to deliver me from my lifelong practice of clutter. However, I am not interested in creating any space that is so meticulously tidy that it makes other people uncomfortable.

If you peek into my office, it's quite clear that I'm not a practitioner of feng shui. Yet I believe in its merit. I believe in it, not because of the Chinese, or the people who I know practice it. I believe in it because of what I understand about the Sabbath. Sabbath is God's word for a people who have a proclivity toward cluttering up their lives with manic activity to fulfill ravenous appetites and unfulfilled needs. Sabbath is God's word for people who, if left to their own devices, would diminish their lives with the clutter of endless busyness and insatiable consumption. Sabbath is for people who clutter their lives so much that they have no space, appetite, or time for God.

In my study of the text, I discovered that Sabbath is not Sunday. In fact, Sabbath is not any day of the week. Sabbath is a component of Creation in which we are invited to repose in the awesome splendor of God. The people who composed the Creator Story included Sabbath as a radical response to the oppressive impositions and dehumanizing expectations designed by the greed and consumption insanity of empire. "The meaning of Sabbath is to celebrate time rather than space. Six days a week we live under the tyranny of things of space; on the Sabbath we try to become attuned to the holiness in time."[71] Sabbath time was a counternarrative to a world that sought only to produce and consume, produce and consume. Sabbath time is a creative moment to save us from ourselves and give us a moment to become preoccupied with our Creator God.

Again, Sabbath is not Sunday, nor any day of the week. Days of the week are human constructs. Days would be days with names or without names. Days are essentially named to facilitate the engines of consumption. We got the term Sunday from the Romans. It was a Roman holiday to commemorate sun worship. Sunday was known as "Sun's day," or Dominica, "Day of God." The Greeks later named the days of the week after the known planets, so Sunday was the Sun's day. Mon-

---

71 Ibid. p. 10

day, named after the moon, was Moon's Day. Tuesday, named after Mars, was Tiu's Day, or Mars' Day. Wednesday, named after Mercury, was Woden's Day, or Mercury Day. Thursday, named after Jupiter, was Thor's Day, or Jupiter Day. Friday, named after Venus, was Freva's Day, or Venus Day. And Saturday, named after Saturn, was Saturn's Day.

> Sabbath time is for people whose lives are at risk of being consumed by the oppressive machinery of produce and consume, produce and consume.

Sunday was never Sabbath and Sabbath was never Sunday because the ancient Egyptians and Babylonians never rested the oppressive machinery of produce and consume, produce and consume. Sabbath becomes a practice of a people who want to be delivered from the vicious cycles of produce and consume. Sabbath was a radical protest against any political and economic machinery that sought to drive people 24/7. Therefore, when the Lord's people were delivered from the Egyptians, a part of their covenant with God was expressed in the commandment, "Remember the Sabbath day, and keep it holy. Six days you shall labor and do all your work, but the seventh day is the Sabbath of the Lord your God. In it you shall do no work . . . For in six days the Lord made the heavens and the earth, the sea, and all that is in them, and rested on the seventh day. Therefore the Lord blessed the Sabbath day and hallowed it."[72]

---

72 Exodus 20:8-11

Sabbath time is for people whose lives are at risk of being consumed by the oppressive machinery of produce and consume, produce and consume. Like feng shui, it is creating a space, or time in life free from the cycle of endless production, competition, and consumption. It is creating a time for God to reenergize us so that we can experience life in more wholesome and healthy ways. We need Sabbath to clear our lives of the clutter created by production and consumption, consumption and production.

Please note the rhythmic cadence in the text! "God ended the work which he had done… God rested on the seventh day from all His work which he had done." And in verse 3, "God rested from all His work which God had created and made." While the things God made didn't rest, God rested. Everything God created kept doing what it was created to do, but God rested. The sun never stopped working, or we wouldn't be here. The planet never stopped working, or we would perish on the first day. The wind never stopped blowing. The waters never stopped flowing—although our recent drought had some thinking otherwise. The birds never stopped flying, fish never stopped swimming, and the plants never stopped growing. All that God created never stopped, but God rested. Rest, in this instance, refers to creative pause.

We need Sabbath time to give us a moment of creative pause. If we are always doing something, always going after something, always reaching for something, always trying to make something, always into something, always up to something, we never allow room for creative pause. We become slaves to what we are doing, slaves to what we are going after, slaves to what we are making, slaves to what we are into, and we never open up space for creative pause. Unlike people made in the image and likeness of God, we duplicate the oppressive practices of our enslavement and without a pharaoh anywhere around, we create one. We become our own slave overseers and push ourselves into making bricks without straw.

Most of us are familiar with pause buttons. Pause buttons are put on devices that are designed to record. We find them on remote controls, or on recording instruments. Pause buttons give us an opportunity to stop a song, to stop a movie, or to stop a show. Pause buttons allow us time to do something else and then get back to the song, movie, or show.

Sabbath time allows us moments to put life on pause. Sometimes things are going too fast, and/or there are things we are just not ready to deal with. How many of us have learned the lesson of trying to force something that's not ready to happen? Sabbath time puts us on pause and delivers us from trying to force things we are not ready for. There is nothing more debilitating to life momentum, or for the momentum of community, than to have to live with something you are not ready for.

I have a dear friend who, when encountering some fascinating dimension of privileged people's lives, often makes the comment, "White folks have everything." Endless access and unfettered privilege has allowed some people, mostly white, to have everything. However, people with a legacy of oppression usually believe they want some of what the oppressors have, only to discover they were not ready for it. While I in no way suggest oppressed people can't handle access and privilege. However, I have observed that some of the things oppressors possess, like endless access and unfettered privileges, oppressed people are not always ready for. For instance, professional black athletes have been known to blow incredible wealth buying things they don't need to impress people they don't like. Perhaps there are some things we have to grow into, and absent of such growth, is a set-up for disaster. A Sabbath pause allows us space to process and prepare for God's Big Next in our lives. I believe that what God prepares, God presets for prosperity.

Creative pause can also be used to rewind some stuff and look at it from a fresh perspective. Everything that God had made was good, but sometimes the stuff we make of what God made is not good and it needs to be rewound and looked at again from another perspective. One of the staple warnings of adolescents and young adults is to slow down. We were cautioned to not move so fast. A senior pastor of my early denominational days was known to say, "Take your time!" We create more space for creativity when we rest. Sabbath provides refreshment for greater creativity.

The text says, "God blessed the seventh day and sanctified." God made the seventh day special, a space for creative perspective. Creative perspective is an opportunity to consider the sacred value of life. Three times the seventh day is mentioned to denote wholeness and completion. We need Sabbath time to give us an opportunity to assess whether or not we have considered the sacred value of life. Sabbath time promotes and encourages the holiness of life, the blessedness of life, and sometimes, the precariousness of life. The question should always be: Has our time been spent promoting wholeness, wellness, and completing our tasks in ways that promote wholesomeness?

When Jesus healed on the Sabbath, he was accused of violating the Sabbath. When his disciples picked corn on the Sabbath, the keepers of religion went into an uproar. Jesus' response to his critics was, "Sabbath was made for man, man was not made for the Sabbath."[73] Jesus condemned any who devalue and demean people for the sake of religious observance. The humanity and wellbeing of people always comes before religious observations. Too often, we can be so into worship that we devalue people. We have been known to be so into our personal worship that we ignore and devalue corporate worship. Church is a space for corporate worship. Corporate worship is sharing the worship of others who are in the same space you are in.

Such creative perspective is critical when living in the context of empire. Empire exists to devalue and demean life. An inevitable to oppression is to devalue life. To maintain the delusion of white supremacy, Christianity was forbidden enslaved

---

[73] Mark 2:27

blacks because it would legitimize black humanity. Oppression operates from the space of the devaluation of life. Pharaoh, Nebuchadnezzar, or Trump, for that matter, never sees people as people, human beings, made in the image and likeness of God. People are only objects to advance the oppressive goals of the economy. Elections are won on the mantra, "It's the economy, stupid!" It's easy to deport people, separate them from their families, commoditize, defile people's sacred spaces; march them into exile, or even bondage, when people are viewed as objects or animals. Sadly, people who are oppressed have a tendency to do to themselves what has been done unto them. We can literally objectify ourselves and put ourselves into positions to be used and discarded when done with.

Sabbath time allows us moments to assess the sacred value in life, and gives us an opportunity to realign our lives with that which is blessed and sanctified. We are given a moment to do in creation what God has done, and that is to bless life and make it special.

Allow me to conclude on this note. While attending school in Texas, I discovered something that is not practiced in California (and it is no longer practiced in Texas.) I encountered the "Blue Law." The Blue Law prohibits the selling of alcoholic beverages on Sundays. It does not say anything about drinking alcoholic beverages. You just could not buy any! If you wanted to have a drink of wine on Sunday, you would have to purchase it before Sunday. (You're probably wondering how I discovered that. Go to college!)

Sabbath time also gives us a moment to engage in creative praise. Notice, the text says, "God rested on the seventh day from all the work which He had done." Creative praise opens up a moment when we consider all the work that God has done and respond with awesome wonder. We don't have to look long, think hard, or dig deep to consider all that God has done. We all know something that the Lord has done.

What once made worship in the Black Church so vibrant and soulful was that black people kept praise simple. We didn't focus on the big things God had done. We didn't need anything big to jumpstart our praise. We praised God for life. We knew that black life was always tenuous, and that our lives could be quickly extinguished by the violent whims and wishes of white people. So, we just praised God for life.

Oh, I can hear the old deacon praying, and the prayer he offered up in praise. While he prayed, we praised. We praised God for waking us up this morning and starting us on our way. We praised God that our bed was not our cooling board, and that our sheet was not our winding sheet. We praised God that the four walls of our room were not the four walls of our grave. We didn't have to have much. We thanked God for food on the table, clothing our backs, and a roof over our heads.

If you really want to set a house of believers off, start praising God for salvation. Sabbath time gave us sacred moments to engage in creative praise. Perhaps we need to quit hiding the fervor of black praise with the crafted veneer of sophistication and praise the Lord. We could quit focusing on what we have done or have not done, and praise God for all He's done! Perhaps we need to take our minds off ourselves altogether and just praise God for the wonderful works He has done. It might be that some of us could use a break from thinking about ourselves. Some of us need a timeout from self-preoccupation. Think about what the Lord has done!

We all know of something that the Lord has done. Think about it! If it's Sunday, that means you've had a whole week. There ought to be something to ignite creative praise. If it's Monday, you have had one day to consider that the Lord made a way for you. If it's Tuesday, you've had two days of blessings and two nights of protection. If it's Wednesday, you've been blessed to make it halfway through the week. If it's Thursday, you've made it over the hump of another week. If it's Friday, join in the song of our hardworking blues ancestors and shout, "The eagle flies on Friday and so do I!" Think about it! Has the Lord kept you for another week? Has the Lord provided for you? Has the Lord blessed you in any kind of way? If so, you ought to praise God for his mighty works. You ought to praise the Lord for what the Lord has done.

I don't know what you are going to do with your Sabbath time, but I'm not going to waste it, trivialize it, bungle it, or blow it! I'm going to fill my Sabbath time in praise to the Lord. I'm going to bless God's name. I'm going to magnify God. I'm going to give God glory! I'm going to exalt the Lord, and lift him up. HALLELUJAH! PRAISE GOD'S NAME!

DISCUSSION MATTERS

1. Are there cluttered areas in your life that inhibit Sabbath time? What are they? How did they develop?

2. Rabbi Herschel identifies the Sabbath as "the sanctification of time." In what ways do we desecrate time?

3. While Christians observe Sundays as a time of worship, what are some ways we could recapture the "holiness" of Sabbath, or create Sabbath time?

4. What would a creative pause do for your life?

5. The Black Lives Matter movement is a protest against a worldview that makes black dispensable, how might Sabbath help us to recapture the value of life, particularly black life?

6. Praise of God has been referred to as a time of sacred "play," have you incorporate playfulness into your Sabbath time? If not, what could it look like?

www.ingramcontent.com/pod-product-compliance
Lightning Source LLC
Chambersburg PA
CBHW050558300426
44112CB00013B/1977